BABY BOOMER TOYS AND COLLECTIBLES

CAROL TURPEN

With Price Guide

77 Lower Valley Road, Atglen, PA 19310

DEDICATION

To my family and toy collecting friends, whose
encouragement gave me the motivation to produce
this book.

PHOTO CREDITS

Bob Conge (Robots and Space Toys) 28 Harper Street Rochester, NY 14607
Barry Brandon (Nutty Mads) 437 N. Nettleton Bonner Springs, KS 66012
Chris Probett (Battery Operated Toys) 8745 Lake Angela Drive San Diego, CA 92119
Joseph Hilton (The Beatles) 216 Epping Road Exeter, NH 03833
John Krupienski (Hanna-Barbera) 5200 Hilltop Drive-AA6 Brookhaven, PA 19015
Bob Vermeulen (Plastic Toys) 10018 Eastlake Drive Fairfax, VA 22032
Ron Smith (Futuristic Cars) 33005 Arlesford Solon, Ohio 44139
Jim/Ayer Comics (Munsters) 28 Main Street Ayer, MA 01432
Howard Harris (Monster Toys) 11184 Roddy Road # 14 San Antonio, TX 78263

Published by Schiffer Publishing, Ltd.
77 Lower Valley Road
Atglen, PA 19310
Please write for a free catalog.
This book may be purchased from the publisher.
Please include $2.95 postage.
Try your bookstore first.

We are interested in hearing from authors
with book ideas on related subjects.

CONTENTS

Acknowledgments

I would like to give special thanks to Bob Conge, John Krupienski, Chris Probett, Joseph Hilton and Barry Brandon. Without their help this book may not have been possible.

Introduction

Any student who makes an exhaustive study, whether physical, spiritual or historical, and fails to share with his fellow man the conclusions arrived at as a result of the special knowledge thus acquired, has wasted his time and effort. Roscoe Carisle d'Armand, writer and kinsman The DeArmond Families of America.

This book was put together for collectors, dealers and "Baby Boomers" everywhere. There are numerous items that are collected by the "Baby Boomers" but this book is basically about the toys of the "Baby Boomers" generation. The word collectibles was added to the title because there are certain items that would not be considered a toy but more of a collectible.

It would be impossible to include every collectible toy of the "Baby Boom" era in this book, so I tried to focus on some of the major areas of collecting.

There are photos of uncommon, hard to find items and also photos of the more common but popular toys that we all had and love to remember.

The "Baby Boom" was a period covering almost two decades when approximately 73 million babies were born in America. According to the Library of Congress, the "Baby Boom" began in 1946 and ended in 1965. This was the largest population explosion in American history. This book covers significant toys manufactured during that period dating from the early fifties to the early seventies.

There may never be another generation that has witnessed as many spectacular events as the "Baby Boomers." This generation watched the first man walk on the moon, saw Ed Sullivan introduce "The Beatles" and cried together when they heard that President John F. Kennedy had been shot.

The boomers were also among the very first ones to own a television set. In the fifties, when television was placed in over 50 million homes, lives were suddenly changed.

Television gave manufacturers a new means of advertising. Realizing that the children of the "Baby Boom" made up the largest portion of the viewing audience, toy manufacturers decided to take advantage of their captive audience by placing toy commercials in just the right places.

Every type of toy imaginable was produced to tempt the boomers and toy commercials brought toy sales to an all time high. The toy salesman's familiar phrase "Be the first in your neighborhood," was beginning to be heard more and more often. This phrase was especially common on Saturdays when boomers were usually found settled in front of the television with a lukewarm cup of Ovaltine watching "Sky King," "Roy Rogers" or a wide range of cartoons.

Tips for New Collectors

New collectors may start out buying everything they can find just to watch their collections rapidly grow, but as they mature in collecting they begin to weed out their collection and start buying only desirable toys in good condition.

Advanced collectors only buy the best and are very selective. These collectors are willing to pay more and get a toy that is in mint condition. They also know the value of a toy is substantially increased if it is in the original box. The vast majority of advanced collectors buy only mint-in-the-box (m.i.b.) toys.

Quantity is not as important as quality. It's better to have a small but very good collection than to have a large collection of undesirable toys.

Terms Frequently Used to Describe the Conditions of the Toys

MIB or MB This stands for mint in box and it is used in describing a toy that is in the original box and has never been played with.

MOC or MC This stands for mint on card and is used to describe a toy that is still packaged on the card that the toy was originally sold on.

NMIB This stands for near mint in box. This describes a toy that is in the original box, but because of slight wear the toy can no longer be described as mint.

MT This stands for mint and is used to describe a toy that is in new condition but is without the original box that the toy came in.

EX This stands for excellent condition and is used to describe a toy that has minor wear and is without the original box.

VG This stands for very good and is used to describe a toy that is in played with condition, but is still worth displaying.

G This stands for good condition and is used to describe a toy that has visible wear.

Poor This term is used to describe a toy that has extensive damage.

CHAPTER ONE
Robots

The term robot is derived from the Czech word "robota," meaning forced labor. A robot is described as any automatically operated machine that replaces human effort. Robots do not necessarily have to resemble humans, or function in a human-like manner, but thanks to the imagination of playwrights and movie makers we've all been able to enjoy their exploits in such films as *The Day the Earth Stood Still, Forbidden Planet* and the series "Lost In Space."

The Japanese in the early 1950s, seeing such an interest in these metal hero's, designed and manufactured toy robots for children to play with.

These brightly colored tin toys initially made for children have become a lost art form. The beauty, color and form are rarely found in our toys of today.

Some people collect robots because of their childhood memories of playing in their rooms for hours with a favorite toy, like "Robby the Robot." Others collect robots because of the beautiful art work and detailed construction of these toys of the past.

For whatever reason, robots remain one of the highest collected toys of the fifties and sixties and have proven to be a profitable investment.

RADICON ROBOT: This robot is one of "The Gang of Four." "The Gang of Four" consist of Radicon, Train, Target and Lavender. This robot was the first robot to feature a wireless remote control. It was made in the fifties and has a lighted chest, lighted eyes and moves in a forward and backward motion.

Mechanized Robot, made in Japan-1950s. Better known as "Robby the Robot," 13½" tall. In 1956 Robby made his debut in the movie "Forbidden Planet" and became the most popular robot of the 1950s. Toy manufacturers realized his popularity and came up with several different versions of Robby, but this battery operated version is the collectors favorite. Beware of reproductions that were produced in 1990.

ROSKO ASTRONAUT: This battery operated robot has the same body style as the mechanized robot Robby. This walking robot features lighted helmet and lighted walkie talkie. The astronaut raises his arm and the walkie talkie begins to beep. It measures 13″ tall and was made in Japan in the fifties.

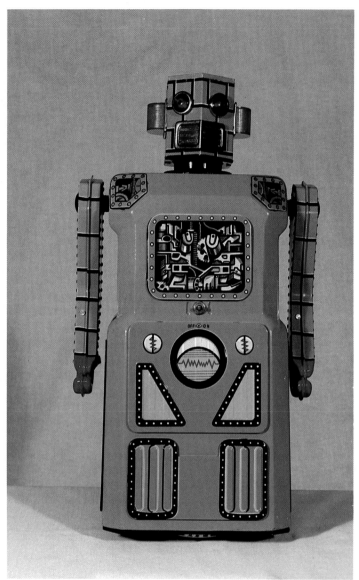

LAVENDER ROBOT: Also known as "Non-Stop Robot," this battery operated robot is another member of "The Gang of Four." Lavender Robot was made in Japan in the 1950s, features swinging arms, light up eyes, mouth, and ears and bump and go action. Lavender Robot measures 15″ tall.

TRAIN ROBOT: This rare robot is part of "The Gang of Four." It was made in Japan in the fifties. Features bump and go action, swinging arms, lighted eyes that alternate and a loud train whistle sound. It measures 15½″ tall.

ROBOTS: The robot pictured on the left walks by remote control. It was made in Japan in the fifties. The robot on the right was made by Linemar. This wind-up robot walks and features engine sound. It measures 6" tall.

CRAGSTAN GREAT ASTRONAUT: This battery operated robot was made in Japan in the sixties. It measures 11½" tall. Features walking action, swinging arms, rotating colors and a lighted TV screen with moving space scenes.

DOOR ROBOT: This remote control robot was made in Japan in the fifties. It measures 9" tall and features a revolving head with two rotating antennas and a band of rotating lights.

9

EXPLO: This all plastic, battery operated robot was made in the sixties. The robot's head and chest explode and the arms fall off. It measures 8¼" tall.

CHIEF ROBOT MAN: This battery operated robot measures 12" tall and was made in Japan in the fifties. It features bump and go action, lighted head, two rotating antennas and it omits sound.

MAN FROM MARS: This all plastic wind-up robot was made in the fifties by Irwin Corp. It measures 11" tall and walks with swinging arms.

RATCHET ROBOT: This all tin, wind-up robot was made in Japan in the fifties. He walks while emitting sparks.

SPACE EXPLORER: This wind-up robot was made in Japan in the fifties. It measures 9¼″ tall. The robot walks as the meter swings back and forth on his chest.

MOON EXPLORER: This battery operated robot measures 18″ tall. It was made in Japan in the sixties. It walks, swings arms, has a lighted head and a moving clock.

FLASHY JIM: This robot was made in Japan in the fifties. It measures 7 ¾" tall and operates by remote control. The robot walks forward and has lighted eyes and mouth.

R-35 ROBOT: This robot measures 7¼" tall and operates by remote control. The robot walks with blinking eyes and swinging arms. It was made in Japan in the fifties.

DINO ROBOT: This battery operated robot was made in Japan in the sixties. It measures 11" tall. The robot walks, then stops as the head opens to reveal a Dinosaur.

ROBOTANK-Z: This battery operated robot was made in Japan in the sixties. It measures 10" tall and 5½" wide. It moves with stop and go action. Features flashing lights, shooting guns and arms move back and forth to operate gears on tank.

THUNDER ROBOT: This battery operated robot measures 11″ tall. It walks as antenna spins, arms raise and guns, located in each hand, fire. It also features blinking lights in eyes and head. This robot was made in Japan in the fifties.

DIRECTIONAL ROBOT: This battery operated robot measures 11″ tall. It features mystery action, and a lighted head that swivels. It was made in Japan in the 1950s.

SPACE ROBOT (X-70): This battery operated robot measures 12½" tall and was made in Japan in the late sixties. It features flashing lights, sound and the head opens to reveal a TV camera.

GEAR ROBOT: This battery operated robot measures 11" tall and was made in Japan in the fifties. This robot features an adjustable dial that controls the speed of the robot. It also features swinging arms, moving antenna, rotating gears and blinking lights.

CRAGSTAN ASTRONAUT: This battery operated robot measures 14" tall. This robot walks then stops to shoot gun, then walks again. This robot was made in the fifties.

SPACE COMMANDER: This battery operated robot measures 10″ tall and was made in Japan in the sixties. It features bump and go actlion and doors that open to reveal firing guns.

COLONEL HAP HAZARD: This battery operated robot was made in the sixties by Marx. It measures 11″ tall. The robot walks with swinging arms, while a lighted, antenna spins around on top of the helmet. This robot usually has the antenna missing, which drastically reduces the value.

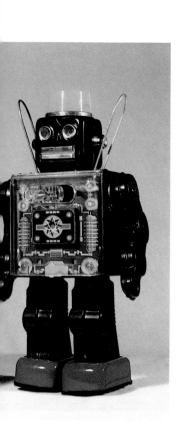

FIGHTING ROBOT: This battery operated robot was made in Japan in the fifties. It features a flashing light on top of head, guns that fire from the chest and swinging arms as it walks. It measures 11¼″ tall.

CRAGSTAN RANGER ROBOT: This battery operated robot is mostly plastic and measures 10½" tall. This robot walks with swinging arms, omits smoke and sound from mouth and has a lighted dome. It was made in Japan in the fifties.

FORKLIFT ROBOT: This battery operated robot measures 12" tall and was made in the 1960s. The robot lifts up a box, walks, then stops and puts the box down.

TV SPACEMAN: This battery operated robot measures 15" tall and was made in Japan in the 1960s. The robot walks with swinging arms, has eyes that rotate and features a TV screen that shows pictures of outer space.

MACHINE ROBOT: This battery operated robot measures 11" tall and was made in Japan in the 1960s. This robot is also referred to as "Turn Signal Robot." Walks with swinging arms, has lighted chest and revolving dome light.

COSMIC FIGHTER: This robot is part tin and part plastic. The robot's head opens revealing a spaceman shooting guns, the head closes when he walks away.

ENGINE ROBOT: This robot features lighted eyes, ears and dome. The robot walks swinging arms and making engine noise while colorful gears rotate.

ELECTRIC ROBOT: This all plastic, battery operated robot was made by Marx. The robot walks with lighted eyes and has a device for sending morse code.

ATTACKING MARTIAN: This battery operated robot was made in the early seventies and measures 9″ tall. The robot walks shooting guns from his chest.

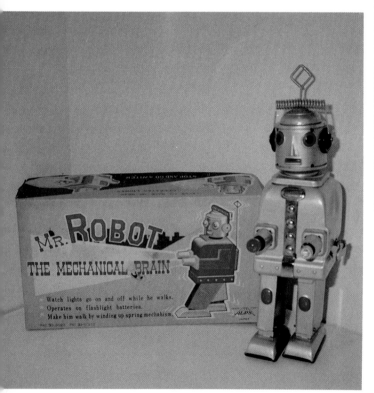

MR. ROBOT THE MECHANICAL BRAIN: This robot is operated by battery and also by a wind-up mechanism. This robot walks with blinking lighted hands.

ZOOMER THE ROBOT: This battery operated robot walks with a lighted head. It was made in the 1950s and measures 9" tall.

MIGHTY ROBOT WITH SPARK: This wind-up robot was made in the 1950s and measures 5½" tall. This small robot, better known as "Sparky," walks along emitting sparks from chest.

SPACEMAN: This wind-up robot was made in the 1950s and measures 8" tall. Arms move and antenna spins as the robot walks.

SPACE SCOUT: This wind-up robot was made in the 1950s and measures 10″ tall. The robot walks forward as a needle on the front of his chest moves.

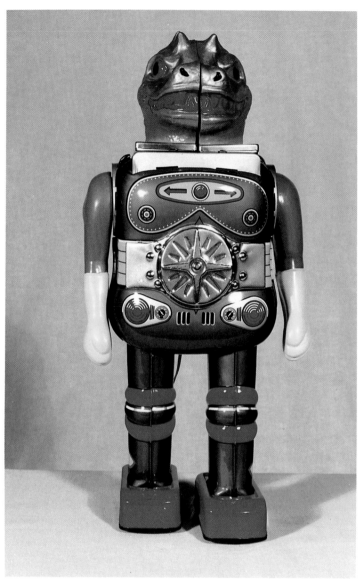

CHANGE MAN ROBOT: This part tin, part vinyl robot was made in the 1960s. It walks along and opens monster head to reveal a green man's head. Measures 13¼″ tall.

MR. PATROL: This battery operated robot was made in the 1960s. It measures 11″ tall. It features a moving dial, a flashing light in chest and it emits a siren sound.

DALEK: This all plastic, battery operated toy was made in 1974 by Marx. Dalek was a robot from the series "Dr. Who."

ROBBIE ROBOT: This all plastic robot was made by Mort Toys in the 1970s. The battery operated robot walks making a click-click sound, moving arms, while lighted eyes blink.

SPACE EXPLORER: This battery operated robot was made in the 1960s. The robot walks as antenna turns and space scenes are shown on his chest. The robot in this photo is missing the antenna.

LOST IN SPACE ROBOT: This battery operated toy was made in the seventies by AHI. It features blinking lights and stop and go action. It measures 10″ tall.

BLINK-A-GEAR ROBOT: This battery operated robot was made in the 1960s. It features blinking eyes, swinging arms and colorful gears which turn and make a machine noise when the robot walks.

TELEVISION SPACEMAN: This wind-up robot measures 7½″ tall and was made in Japan in the sixties. The robot rolls along wobbling from side to side, while antenna rotates and space scenes are shown from TV screen located on the robot's chest.

CHAPTER TWO
Space Toys

In the 1960s when manned lunar exploration became a reality, it opened the door to exploration in regions far from Earth. Space exploration provides man with the ability to unshackle himself from his native planet, and it represents a new dimension of thought and achievement.

Long before any real accomplishments had been made in space flight, comic strips such as "Buck Rogers" and movies such as "Forbidden Planet" kept children's imaginations filled with the mystery and excitement of the unknown.

Toy manufacturers realized that children were fascinated by outer space and soon rockets, spaceships and space vehicles of every kind imaginable were produced for children. The futuristic space toys that were produced in the 1940s and 1950s were designed solely from the imagination. A lot of space vehicles were fashioned after the ones used by fictional characters such as Flash Gordon, Tom Corbett and Buck Rogers. Character related toys are always a wise investment and this applies to any type of space toy.

One highly collectible space vehicle made to look like the one in the movie *Forbidden Planet* is Robby's Space Patrol. This toy is not desirable because of it's actions or looks, but simply because few were produced. The toy was unlicensed and M.G.M. quickly put a stop to the production. It is believed that only about two hundred of them were made.

In the 1950s, when the United States was just beginning to invest large amounts of money into space programs, the Japanese were investing their money by producing space toys to sell to the United States.

MAN MADE SATELLITE: This all tin friction toy was made in Japan. It measures 4" in diameter and has four spring antennas. This toy was made to resemble a Soviet satellite, known as Sputnik 1.

RENDEZVOUS 7&8: This battery operated toy was made in Japan in the 1960s and is 15" long. This toy consists of two separate parts connected with a white extension plug, which also acts as an on and off switch. This toy moves forward and features lighted dome and a rocket that emits space sounds.

RADICON SPACE PATHFINDER: Made in Japan in the 1960s, this remote control toy is sound activated. Although the toy is battery operated, the remote takes no batteries and is used to make a clicking noise that the toy will respond to.

Although the Japanese were not involved in space exploration at the time, they did turn out some of the most popular space toys. The Japanese space vehicles with blinking lights, rotating antennas and opening doors were purely fictional.

In the early 1960s scientists and engineers began designing spacecraft for NASA and space toys began to take on a more realistic appearance. As more and more NASA space programs evolved, so did realistically copied space toys. A great many space toys were derived from real space events, such as the Friendship 7. On February 20, 1962, astronaut John H. Glenn Jr. became the first American to circle the Earth three times. He accomplished the feat in a spacecraft known as the Friendship 7.

The Friendship 7 toy was only one of many that were patterned after the real thing. Space capsules such as Mercury and Gemini also had small, somewhat realistic toy versions produced.

The very early satellites such as Sputnik 1, which the Soviet Union launched in 1957, were seldom copied by toy manufacturers. One toy that came close to resembling the Sputnik 1, is a fairly uncommon toy made in Yonezawa, Japan, called 'Man Made Satellite.'

The battery-operated wheeled space vehicles, with all the great actions and beautiful colored lights, were probably the favorite among children of the 1950s and

1960s. Toys such as these helped children travel along the surface of many a distant planet. In the 1950s and early 1960s, such a vehicle did not yet exist in the real world, so toy designers created their own imaginary versions of what this vehicle would look like. A majority of them resembled army tanks, but some looked a lot like automobiles. There is even one that looks like a Volkswagen.

It was not until July 30, 1971, that astronauts explored the surface of the moon from the seats of the first Lunar Rover vehicle. Astronauts David R. Scott, James R. Irwin and Alfred M. Worden rode the Lunar Rover a total of 18 hours and 36 minutes and collected approximately 170 pounds of surface samples.

Some people think space exploration is a waste of time and money. These people probably never read comic strips such as "Buck Rogers" or grew up as a child who never missed an episode of "Lost in Space" and most certainly never played with space toys.

Space toys were not of interest to all children of the 1950s and 1960s of course. Space toys were for the child with a vivid imagination who had hidden dreams of seeking out the unknown. These children probably had ancestors who supported the travels of Columbus, marveled at Jules Verne, and never once laughed at Edison's inventions.

OUTER SPACE PATROL: Made in Japan, this friction toy measures 8″ long. It features an astronaut that swings from side to side as sparks flash from the rear window.

ZEROID ACTION SET: Made by Ideal in the late 1960s, the Zeroid robots were battery operated and sold individually as well as in sets containing different accessories. This is only one of the various sets produced.

ORBIT EXPLORER WITH AIRBORNE SATELLITE: Made in Japan in the 1950s, this wind-up toy measures 9″ long. It features an astronaut with a TV camera that rotates from side to side, revolving antenna and floating satellite.

SPACE REFUEL STATION: Made in the 1950s, this battery operated toy measures 15″ tall and has flashing lights, revolving antenna and space sound. Toy rolls around, stops and lifts up while revolving in place.

SONICON ROCKET: This tin battery operated toy was made in Japan in the 1950s. It runs in all directions and changes directions when you blow a whistle, clap your hands, or make any type of loud noise. It came with a plastic antenna that is usually missing from the toy.

CRAGSTAN SPACE TANK: This all tin friction toy was made in Japan in the 1950s. As it rolls, the spaceman flips over, turning into a spinning ball. It is 6" long.

RADAR TANK: Made in the late 1950s, this battery operated toy measures 8″ long, has non-fall action, rotating antenna, blinking dome light and space sound.

MOON DETECTOR: Made in Japan in the 1960s, this battery operated toy is mostly tin, with a plastic rotating antenna and plastic domes both in front and in back. It has feelers that move up and down, flashing lights and it runs forward and reverse.

APOLLO-II AMERICAN EAGLE LUNAR MODULE: This battery operated toy was made in Japan in the sixties. It features flashing lights, revolving antenna, lunar sound, stop and go action and an opening and closing hatch that reveals astronaut inside.

FRIENDSHIP 7: This friction toy was made in Japan in the 1960s. This toy features a tin astronaut. When you roll it, sparks shoot from the engines.

MOON TRAVELER APOLLO-Z: Made in Japan in the late 1960s, this battery operated toy has stop and go action, jet sound and blinking lights. As it slowly elevates, the nose cone pulls away from the capsule.

SUPER APOLLO SPACE CAPSULE: Made in Japan in the 1960s, this battery operated toy is 9″ tall, has stop and go actions, and revolves as its two hatches open.

SPACE PATROL: The name Space Patrol was given to several different space toys in the fifties and sixties, but the most famous and valuable of all the different variations, was the "Robby" Space Patrol.

SPACE PATROL X-11: Made in Japan in the 1960s, this battery operated toy features non-fall action, rotating antenna, space sound and doors on top that open to reveal a lighted dome.

SPACE PATROL TANK: Made in Japan in the 1960s, the battery operated tank bounces along, has revolving antenna and a lighted dome which reveals space scenes.

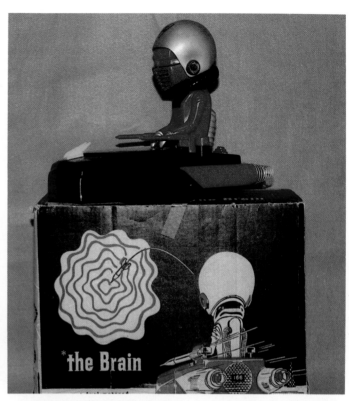

MOON EXPLORER: Made in the late 1960s, this battery operated toy has mystery action, lights that spin under a transparent opening in the roof, flashing light on top and a vinyl astronaut that moves under the dome. It also makes space noises.

THE BRAIN-"Z MAN": Made in Japan in the 1950s, this programmable toy could be directed to go in different directions by sliding down the helmet and pushing buttons on top of its head.

LUNAR TRANSPORT: Made in the 1960s, this part tin, part plastic remote control toy has rotating antenna, multi-colored working gears and flashing cabin lights.

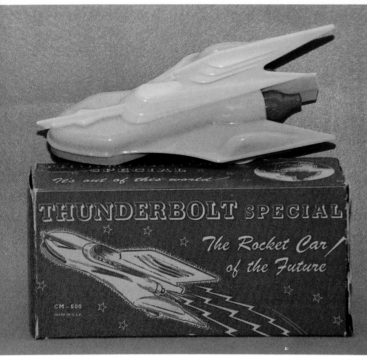

SPACE FIGHTER: This friction toy was made in Japan in the 1950s and measures 18½″ long. The toy rolls along with guns, located in the front, shooting out sparks and sparks also coming from the exhaust area. Two tin astronauts are located under the dome.

THUNDERBOLT SPECIAL: Advertised as 'The Rocket Car of the Future,' this multi-colored plastic toy was made in the U.S.A. in the 1950s and rolled on wheels.

MOON ORBITER: Made in Japan in the 1960s, this 4″ vehicle is battery operated and runs along on a tin litho track using magnets to attach the vehicle.

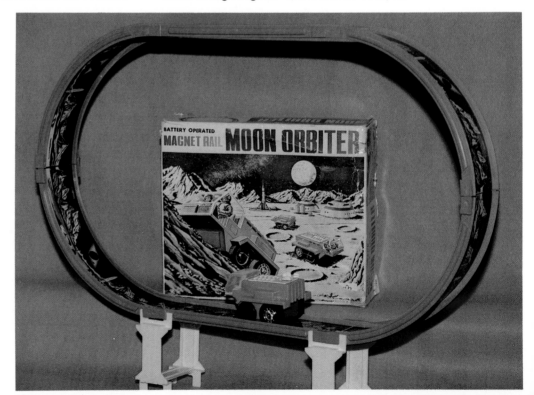

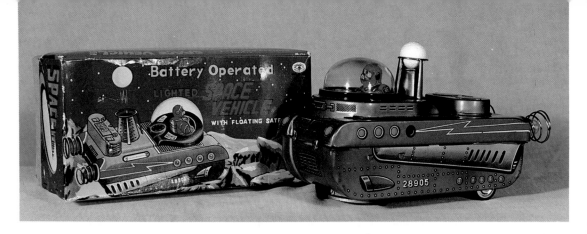

LIGHTED SPACE VEHICLE: Made in Japan in the 1960s, this battery operated toy has flashing rear lights, bump and go action and has air coming out the top to keep a small white ball floating in the air.

SUPER MOON PATROLLER Made in Japan in the 1960s, this battery operated toy features stop and go actions, flashing lights, engine noises and two hatches that open to reveal firing guns on one side and an astronaut on another.

SPACE SHIP X-5: Made in Japan in the 1960s, this battery operated toy has bump and go action, flashing lights and makes a beep-beep sound.

33

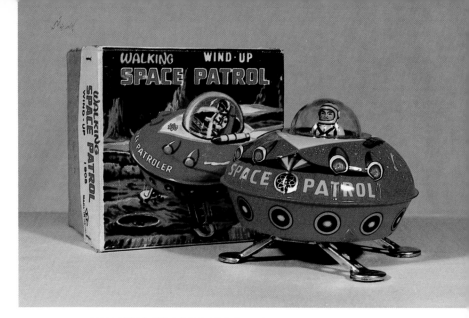

WALKING SPACE PATROL: Made in Japan in the 1960s, this tin wind-up toy walks forward on four legs. It measures 5″ in diameter.

SPACE PATROL R-10: This battery operated tin toy was made in Japan in the 1960s. It has lights that flash from a clear box located in the back seat. When it moves forward it makes a space sound.

U.S.A.-NASA GEMINI: Made in Japan in the 1960s, this battery operated toy has non-fall action, rotating antenna and flashing lights. This is only one of several versions of this toy. The fact that this toy has two astronauts in the cockpit, instead of the usual one, makes it a great deal more valuable. Two astronauts are very uncommon for this toy.

CAPSULE 5: This battery operated toy was made in Japan in the 1960s and is 10½" long by 7" tall. The astronaut moves up and down while lights flash and space sounds are emitted. It features mystery action.

U.S.A.-NASA APOLLO: Made in Japan in the 1960s, this battery operated toy has non-fall action, rotating astronaut and flashing lights.

MAGIC COLOR DOME MERCURY EXPLORER: Made in Japan in the 1960s, this battery operated toy has non-stop action, a jet engine sound, a rotating propeller and has red and blue colored lights that alternate through the dome. It measures 8″ long.

MISSILE BOAT-810: This all tin boat was made in Japan in the 1950s and measures 12″ long. This toy operates with a crank wind-up, has propellers that spin and a robot for a driver.

NEW SPACE CAPSULE: Made in Japan, this battery operated toy is 10″ long, has bump and go action, flashing lights and a hatch that opens to reveal an astronaut with a TV camera.

BUMP 'N GO SPACE EXPLORER: Made in Japan in the 1950s. This was a tin litho with crank wind and bump and go action. When it moves an astronaut moves back and forth while pistons move in and out.

MAGIC COLOR MOON EXPRESS: Made in Japan in the 1960s, this battery operated toy has non-stop action, has alternating green and red lights that appear under the dome and makes space noises. Moon Express and Mercury Explorer are very similar and both were manufactured by T.P.S. of Japan.

LOST IN SPACE MODEL—CYCLOPS: The Lost in Space model (model number 419) featuring the Cyclops was made by Aurora in the sixties.

LOST IN SPACE HALLOWEEN COSTUME: This Halloween costume was made in 1966 by Ben Cooper.

SPACE ORBITESTOR: This battery operated toy was made in Japan for the F. E. White Company in 1969. The toy is all plastic and measures 8½″ long. The space scooter rolls along with flashing lights, then stops automatically and releases a flying saucer.

FLYING JEEP: This friction toy was made in Japan in the fifties. When rolled, the two colorful propellers turn, going in opposite directions.

THE FLOATING SATELLITE: Made in Japan in the late 1950s, this toy featured a battery operated motor which allows a ball to float in the air and stay up while you shot at it with a gun that was provided.

SPACE DOG: This wind-up toy was made in Japan in the fifties and measures 7 ¾" long. His mouth opens and closes, ears go up and down, and eyes roll as he wobbles back and forth. Sparks are emitted from window located on back. The antenna is also an on and off switch.

CHAPTER THREE
Monster Toys

Without a doubt, the most famous monster of all time is Frankenstein. Although the earliest filming of *Frankenstein* was accomplished in 1910 by Thomas Edison, the most memorable performance was that of Boris Karloff. Universal Pictures released this version of the *Frankenstein* movie, starring Boris Karloff, in 1931. Through the years the name Frankenstein has always brought to mind the Boris Karloff portrayal.

In order to become this frightening but somehow pitiful looking monster, Karloff had to endure many hardships. Every morning before shooting could begin, Karloff had to sit for three-and-a-half hours while makeup was applied. Then, with putty on his eyelids and extremely heavy boots on his feet, Karloff battled the hot California sun while wearing thick quilting under his costume.

Frankenstein's great popularity inspired toy manufacturers to create toy versions of the monster and in the sixties several Frankenstein toys were produced. A Japanese toy manufacturer came out with two rather comical versions of the toy. They were called Frankenstein Monster and Mod Monster. The battery operated toys measured 13" tall, were mostly vinyl and cloth and were mounted on a tin base. The toys were very much the same except for the clothes.

Both toys feature a monster who makes a walking motion, then drops his pants to reveal boxer shorts. Realizing his pants have fallen, his face lights up with embarrassment.

In the 1950s a toy manufacturer by the name of Louis Marx came out with one of the most popular Frankenstein toys ever made. With this toy, Marx came very close to capturing the look of the Boris Karloff Frankenstein. This battery operated toy measures 12" tall and is known as Walking Frankenstein. Operated by remote control, this toy features four buttons which allow him to walk, move his arms up and down, open and close his arms and bend at the waist.

Opposite page:
WALKING FRANKENSTEIN: Made by Marx in the 1950s, this remote control toy is popular with monster toy collectors, battery operated toy collectors and robot collectors. He walks, bends at the waist and picks up objects. This toy is seldom found in working order.

FRANKENSTEIN: This model kit was made by Aurora in 1961 and was the first model kit that Aurora produced featuring famous monsters.

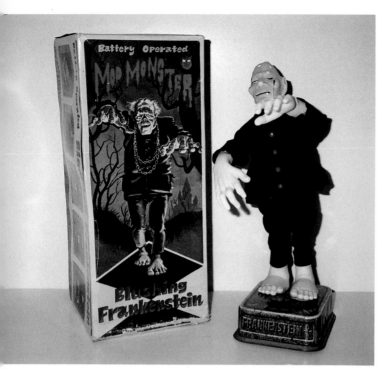

The monster items, being in such demand, prompted Colgate-Palmolive to come out with bubble bath containers shaped into full length monster figures. These bubble bath containers, known as Soakys, have become very collectible. Of all the Soaky monster containers that were made, The Creature From the Black Lagoon seems to be the hardest one to find and therefore the most valuable.

Year after year new monsters are created and I am sure the monsters of the past must have been very frightening in their day, but they seem mild in comparison to the monsters of the nineties. Several toys have recently been designed and then recalled as soon as they hit the toy store shelves because they were too frightening for young children.

Let's face it, what child would want to go to bed sleeping next to a Freddy Krueger doll?

MOD MONSTER: A Japanese toy manufacturer came out with two rather comical versions of this toy. They were called Frankenstein Monster and Mod Monster. The battery operated toys measured 13″ tall, were mostly vinyl and cloth and were mounted on a tin base. The toys were very much the same except for the clothes. Both toys feature a monster who makes a walking motion, then drops his pants to reveal boxer shorts. Realizing his pants have fallen, his face lights up with embarrassment.

The Walking Frankenstein by Marx, was also featured in a popular 1960 TV series called "The Munsters." "The Munsters" starred Fred Gwenn as the comical Frankenstein father, Herman Munster. In one episode, Herman Munster saw the toy and thought it resembled him so closely that it must be his new son.

The popularity of "The Munsters" enticed toy manufacturers to produce a variety of Munster toys. These Munster toys are highly collectible among the baby boomers who grew up watching the weekly show.

Other well known monsters are Wolfman, Dracula, The Hunchback of Notre Dame, The Creature From the Black Lagoon and The Mummy. In the 1960s Aurora came out with model kits of each of these. Some of the most sought after monster models are the ones featuring monsters driving hot rods. Around 1964 Aurora came out with Dracula's Dragster, The Mummy's Chariot, Frankenstein's Flivver and Wolfman's Wagon. In 1966 Aurora came out with two of the most desirable monster model kits featuring hot rod driving monsters. One is King Kong's Thronester and the other is Godzilla's Go Cart.

Another monster model that is very desirable is Gigantic Frankenstein. This two foot model of Frankenstein has been given the nick name Big Frankie.

FAMOUS MONSTERS AND FRANKENSTEIN'S FLIVVER: The Hunchback of Notre Dame and The Creature from the Black Lagoon were both model kits that were made by Aurora in 1963. Frankenstein's Flivver is pictured in front of these model kits. The Flivver was made by Aurora in 1964 and was the first kit made by Aurora to feature the Monster hot rod.

WOLFMAN: This glow in the dark monster model was made in the early seventies by Aurora. This later version of monster model kits is not worth nearly as much as the earlier monster models released by Aurora in the sixties.

THE MUMMY: This model kit was one of the Famous Monster models that Aurora made. It was made in 1963.

WOLFMAN'S WAGON: This model was made by Aurora in 1964. This is one of six kits that Aurora made featuring monsters driving hot rods.

MONSTER SCENES: The Monster Scenes model kits were made by Aurora in 1971. The Monster Scene that is most wanted by collectors is Vampirella.

MONSTER SCENES AND MONSTERS OF THE MOVIES: This Monster Scene model kit was made in 1971 by Aurora, featuring Dr. Deadly. The Monsters of the Movies model kit was made in 1975 by Aurora and featured The Creature From the Black Lagoon.

MONSTER SCENES—VAMPIRELLA: Vampirella is the most sought after Monster Scene. Monster Scenes were made by Aurora in 1971.

LAND OF THE GIANTS—THE SNAKE SCENE: "The Land of the Giants" was a television show that aired in the sixties. This model kit was made by Aurora in 1968. It was made to represent a scene from the weekly show.

MONSTER SOAKYS: Made in the 1960s by Colgate-Palmolive, these plastic monsters contained bubble baths. The Mummy is on the left, Wolfman is on the right.

FRANKENSTEIN MONSTER: This battery operated toy was made in the sixties by Rosko and measures 13" tall. He makes a walking motion by moving his arms back and forth, then drops his pants to reveal boxer shorts. His face lights up with embarrassment.

THE MIGHTY KONG: This remote control toy was made in the 1950s by Marx. It measures 11" tall. It walks and beats its chest as it roars, opening and closing its mouth.

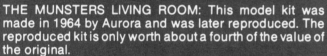

THE MUNSTERS LIVING ROOM: This model kit was made in 1964 by Aurora and was later reproduced. The reproduced kit is only worth about a fourth of the value of the original.

GRANDPA MUNSTER HAND PUPPET: This hand puppet was made in 1964 by Ideal and features a vinyl head and cloth body.

THE MUNSTERS CARD GAME: The Munster Card Game was made in 1964 by Milton Bradley Company.

MUNSTER DOLLS: Made by Remco in 1964. Left to right, Lilly Munster, Herman Munster and Grandpa.

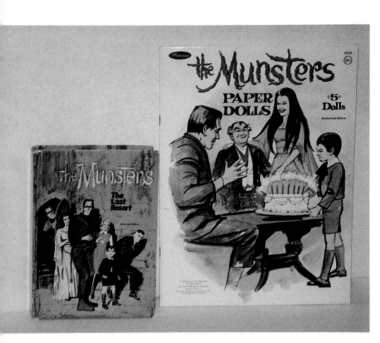

THE MUNSTERS, THE LAST RESORT AND THE MUNSTERS PAPER DOLLS: The Munsters book, on the left was made in 1966 by Whitman and The Munsters Paper Dolls on the right were also made by Whitman in 1966.

GRANDPA MUNSTER'S DRAG-U-LA AND MUNSTER KOACH: These two model kits were made in 1964 by AMT and licensed by Kayro-Vue.

THE ADDAMS FAMILY HAUNTED HOUSE: This model kit was made in the sixties by Aurora. It is made to look like the house that was in the weekly series "The Addams Family."

LURCH: This toy was made by Remco in 1964 and features rooted hair and a jointed neck. The character Lurch was the butler in the 1960s television series, "The Addams Family."

GOMEZ HAND PUPPET: This toy was made in 1964 by Ideal and features a vinyl head and cloth body. Gomez was one of the main characters in "The Addams Family."

HAMILTON'S INVADERS: These plastic play sets were made in the sixties by Remco. Hamilton is the large green bug located in the right hand corner of the photo on the bottom. These bugs operate with spring motors.

WITCH PITCH: This toy was made in 1970 by Parker Brothers. The top of the witch house spins around while you take turns trying to pitch plastic chips in the open window.

FAMOUS MONSTERS REPRODUCTIONS: The mold that was used to produce the original Famous Monster figures was sold and reproductions are now being made. The colors are not the same as the Marx originals. These two figures are reproductions.

FAMOUS MONSTERS: These plastic figures were made in the sixties by Marx. Marx produced six famous monsters: the Creature From the Black Lagoon, Frankenstein, Hunchback, Wolfman, Mummy and The Phantom of the Opera.

GROOVY GHOULIES: These plastic figures were part of a set that was made in the early seventies. "The Groovy Ghoulies" was an animated TV show that came out in the seventies.

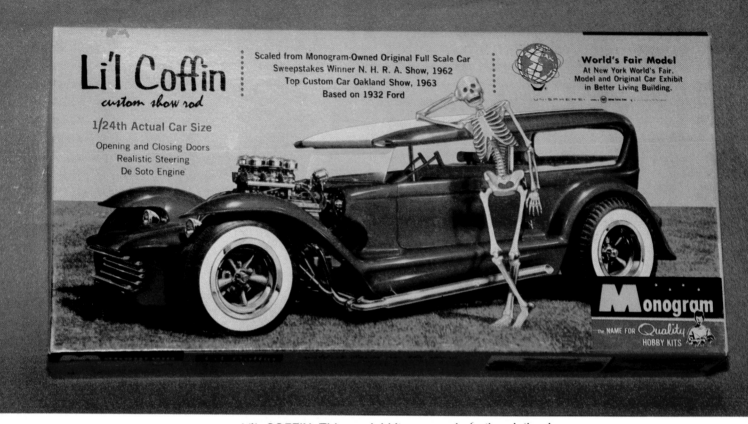

LI'L COFFIN: This model kit was made in the sixties by Monogram and based on an actual car that was on exhibit at the New York Worlds Fair.

MONSTER VITAMINS: These vitamins were made in 1972 by Bristol-Myers.

ROARING GORILLA: This battery operated toy comes with a gun and darts. Shoot the gorillas chest and it roars and raises it's arms.

GORILLA: A battery operated, remote controlled toy that walks and roars while swinging it's arms, and opening and closing it's lighted mouth.

CREEPLE PEEPLE THINGMAKER: In the sixties Mattel came out with kits called Thingmakers. These do-it-yourself mini-factories came with molds, tubes of plastic (called goop) and small electric heaters. The plastic was formed into everything from worms to flowers. This thingmaker kit made monster-like figures that you could place on the end of a pencil.

JIRAS: This battery operated toy walks, moves it's arms, opens it's mouth, growls, and breathes smoke. It's eyes and mouth light up. It was made in Japan.

FORD FAIRLANE 500: This all tin, friction car was made in Japan in the late fifties. It measures 9½″ long.

CHAPTER FOUR
Futuristic Toy Cars and Other Vehicles

There are four very important things to consider when investing in toy cars: size, age, detail and popularity. The large well detailed toy is what the collectors look for.

Cars that are popular on the road will usually be equally popular as a toy. This rule would not apply to futuristic toy cars, however, because most of these were purely imaginary and were not made to represent actual cars.

The size of a toy car does not always determine the value. One example is a Mercedes that was made in the seventies. This particular toy measures almost two feet long but only sells for around $150 in mint-in-the-box (m.i.b.) condition because of the large number of them that exist.

When determining the age of a toy car, be sure to study the reproductions that are currently on the market so they will be easily recognized. There are many tin cars which have been manufactured within the past three years to look like the tin cars of the fifties and have even come in an old looking box. These pretenders are only worth around fifteen to twenty dollars, so do not be fooled.

When investing in toy cars, always remember to consider the condition. Whether it is toy cars or any other toy, the condition is always one of the most important things to look for. Never buy a toy that is not in excellent to near mint condition and whenever possible, try to purchase toys that are mint-in-the-box.

FIREBIRD III: A battery operated toy was made in Japan in the 1960s. This red and yellow version was made by Alps of Japan and measures 11½" long. It featured mystery action, flashing engine lights and engine noises.

FIREBIRD II: The Firebird II is the rarest of the three Firebirds. This toy was copied after the gas turbine powered car that General Motors hand built as an experimental model for show room exhibition in the fifties. This 8½" long friction car was made in Japan by Ashahi.

FIREBIRD: This battery operated toy is one of a series of three Firebird toy cars produced. It was made in Japan in the fifties. This toy was patterned after the Firebird XP-21 that GM built in 1954. The Firebird was America's first gas turbine automobile.

FIREBIRD III: The red and white version of the Firebird III was made by Alps of Japan in the 1960s for Cragstan and measures 11½″ long. It also had mystery action, flashing lights and engine noises.

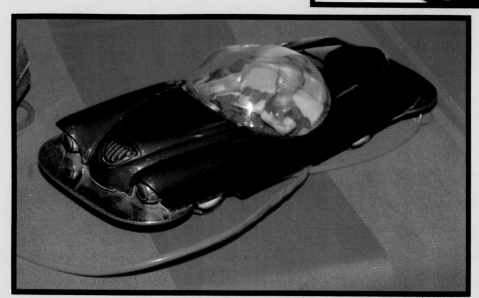

DREAM CAR: This futuristic toy car is operated by remote control. It was made in the 1950s by Linemar and measures 12″ long.

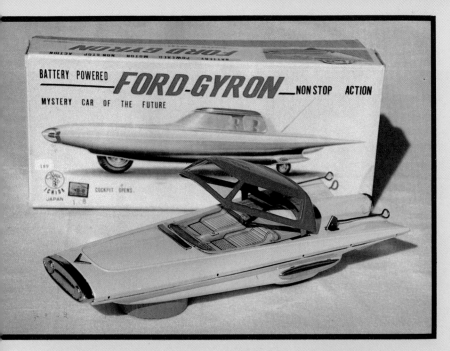

FORD GYRON: This battery operated toy was made in Japan by Ichida in the 1960s and measures 11″ long. The cockpit opens and the antennas located on the back of the car raise up.

DREAM CAR: This 15″ long dream car was made in the fifties by Yonezawa of Japan.

BUICK LE SABRE: This friction car was made in Japan in the fifties. It measures 8″ long.

LINCOLN XL: This friction car was made in Japan in the fifties and measures 8″ long.

FUTURISTIC CAR: This friction car was made in Japan in the fifties and measures 8″ long.

BUICK PHANTOM DREAM CAR: This 12″ long friction toy was made in Germany by Tipp & Company.

THE LINDBERG: This car was made in the early sixties. It was a battery operated, motorized model produced exclusively for Sears.

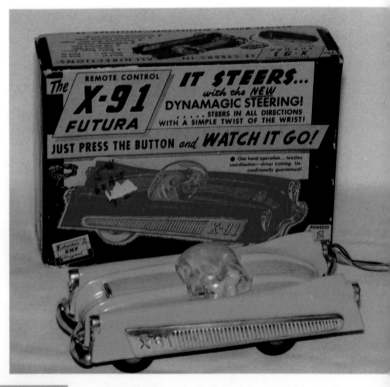

X-91 FUTURA: This all plastic, battery operated toy is guided by remote control and features a steering device attached to the remote control unit.

FUTURISTIC CARS: These two futuristic cars were made in the fifties by Tootsietoy and measure 6″ long.

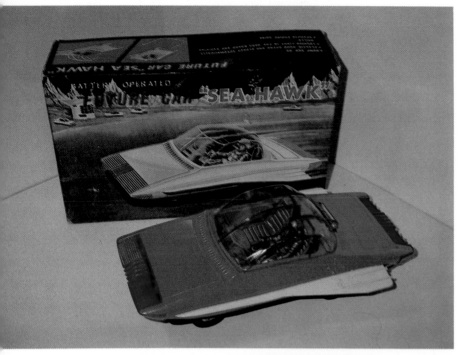

"SEA HAWK": This battery operated toy was made in Japan in the sixties and measures 11½" long. It features bump and go action, turning light in the dash board and radiator, engine noise and a canopy that opens and closes automatically.

ELECTROMOBILE: This battery operated car was made in Japan in the 1950s, has working headlights and an on and off switch that is located on the side of the car. It measures 8" long.

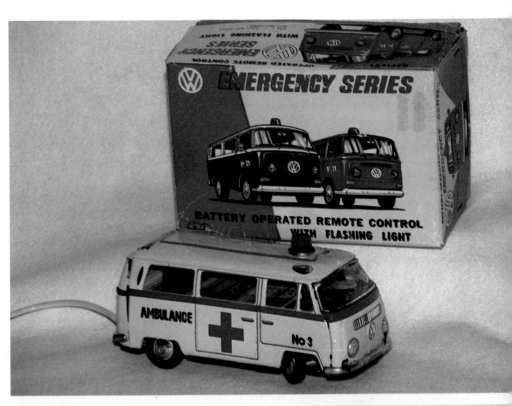

VOLKSWAGEN-EMERGENCY SERIES: This battery operated bus was made in Japan in the early seventies and operates by remote control. The toy features a flashing light and a steering device attached to the remote control that enables the bus to go in any direction.

CITROEN DS19: This all tin car was made in Japan in the 1960s and is friction powered.

DUNE BUGGY: This part tin, part plastic, battery operated toy was made in the early seventies. It does a wheel stand and features roaring engine sound.

DUNE BUGGY WITH CAMPER TRAILER: This wind-up toy was made in the early seventies. The spare tire located on the dune buggy is used as a winding device.

WIKING VOLKSWAGENS: These all plastic toys were made in Germany in 1961. They measure 2″ long. There are newer versions of these same cars on the market, but the colors are different.

SMOKING VOLKSWAGEN: This battery operated toy was made in Japan in the early seventies. It features mystery actions and smoke. It also stops and shakes up and down, as if the car were experiencing engine trouble. The Smoking Volkswagen measures 10½″ long.

KING SIZE VOLKS-
WAGEN: This battery
operated toy was made
in Japan in the sixties
and features a sun roof
that opens and closes
and a visible operating
engine.

BUDDY L TRUCK AND
CAMPER: This toy was
made by Buddy L in the
early sixties. The metal
truck came with a plastic
camper, fold down stairs
and a plastic boat
located on top of the
camper. The camper and
boat are both removable.

RAGGEDY ANN AND ANDY CAMPER: This toy was made in the early seventies by Buddy L. It features a metal camper with a plastic bottom, plastic figures of Raggedy Ann and Andy, a dog and a boat.

MUSICAL CADILLAC CAR: This battery operated toy was made in Japan in the 1950s. Located on the side of the car is an on and off switch. When the Musical Cadillac is turned on, the car rolls along playing music.

FORD THUNDERBIRD COUPE: This friction car was made in Japan in the late 1960s and features an opening door located on the drivers side.

SCHUCO 5503: This "Elektro-Phanomenal" car was made by Schuco in the fifties and is battery operated.

CORVETTE MODEL ASSEMBLY KIT: This all plastic car was made in the sixties by Ideal. It can be assembled and taken apart over and over again. It features working headlights.

SOUND BUS: This battery operated toy was made in Japan in the late sixties. It has non-stop action and makes a loud horn-like sound.

TOM AND JERRY ROADSTER: This battery operated toy was made in Japan in the late sixties. It is part tin and part plastic. Because this toy features Tom and Jerry it is highly collectible.

BMW ISETTA: This all tin friction toy was made in Japan in the fifties.

VOLKSWAGEN BUS: This battery operated bus was made in Japan in the sixties. It travels in a figure eight pattern.

CADILLAC: This friction car was made in Japan in the sixties and measures 10″ long.

FORD MUSTANG: This battery operated Mustang fastback was made in Japan in the early seventies and features non-fall, bump-'n-go and mystery action. This was one of a series of three cars that were made and all three had the same actions.

U-TURN CADILLAC: This battery operated car has an automatic u-turn action. The driver puts his arm out the window to signal for a turn. It features a light located on the hood that lights with every u-turn.

GO-KART: This toy was made in Germany by Schuco. It is a wind-up toy.

1957 CHEVY: This wind-up plastic AMF/Wen-Mac '57 Chevy measures 12" long. Red is a common color for this toy. This toy also came in yellow and blue. Both are very hard colors to find.

This battery operated car measures 7″ long. It was made in Japan.

PROMOTIONAL CARS: These plastic, friction cars were promotional items given out by car dealerships. Left: 1964 Thunderbird Right: 1960 Desoto

TONKA SURBURBAN PUMPER: This fire engine was made by Tonka in the late fifties. It came with a small metal fire hydrant that is sometimes missing.

JOHNNY LIGHTENING POWER COMPRESSOR: This Johnny Lightening Power Compressor set was made by Topper in 1970. This set is the least valuable of all the Johnny Lightening boxed sets.

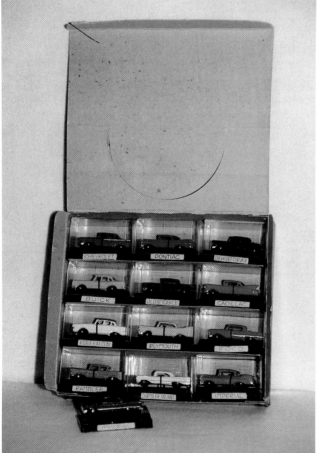

AUTHENTIC MODEL CAR SERIES: These die-cast cars were made in Japan in the late fifties. They came in individual plastic show cases. Each car measures 2″ long.

THE GREEN HORNET'S BLACK BEAUTY: This die-cast Corgi toy was made in 1966 by Playcraft Toys Limited. It comes with plastic missiles and plastic radar scanners.

MONKEEMOBILE: This die-cast car was made in the sixties. It was available in two sizes, the small one was Corgi Jr. and the larger version was a Corgi. Made in Great Britain by Playcraft Toys Ltd.

DINKY KIT: This metal model was one of the last items that was produced by Dinky. They were not very popular and were made for only a short time.

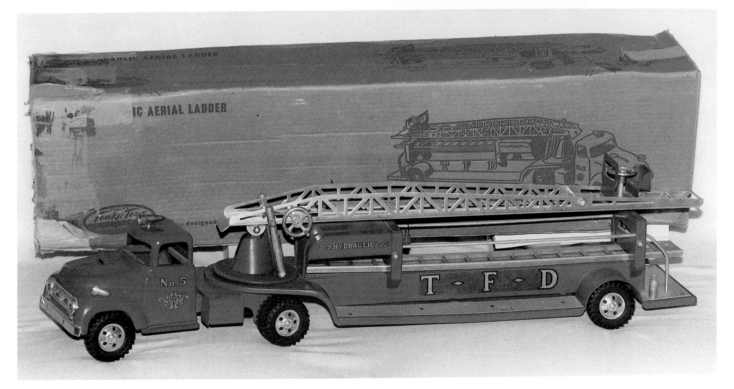

HYDRAULIC AERIAL LADDER: This toy was made by Tonka in the late fifties.

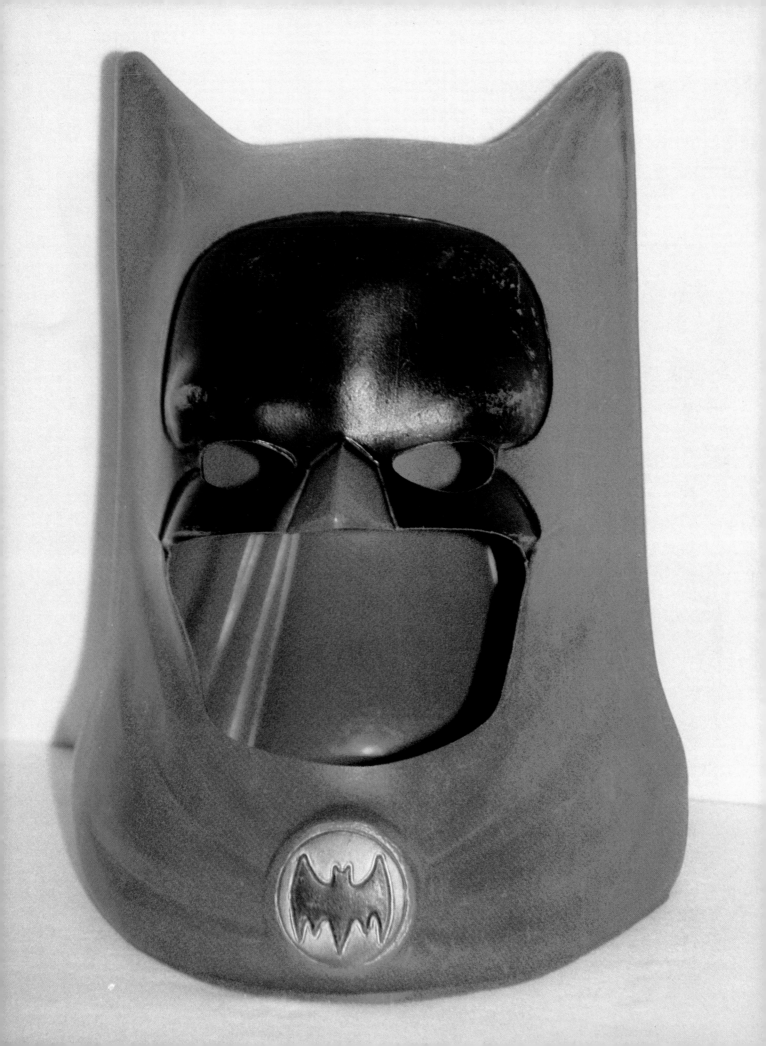

CHAPTER FIVE
Plastic Toys

BIG SHOT: This battery operated toy was made by Marx in the 1960s. Big Shot had a missile firing cannon that could be raised, lowered and fired at the push of a button.

Opposite page:
BATMAN HELMET: This plastic helmet was made in 1966 by Ideal. It was sold with a full length cape (not pictured).

PLAYMOBILE: This battery operated toy was
manufactured by Deluxe Reading in the 1960s. It has a
realistic appearance and the dashboard comes equipped
with windshield wipers, turn signals that light up, a horn
and a key to start the motor.

JOHNNY EXPRESS: This remote control toy was made
by Topper in the 1960s. It goes forward and in reverse,
turns left and right, couples and has variable speeds.

TV JET: This toy was produced by Deluxe Reading during the 1960s and has a TV screen that shows a full color moving picture which represents an aerial view of a jet plane flying over factories, boat docks, train yards, etc. There are 12 different dials and controls, as well as two plastic darts that fire from the top. It is battery operated.

BIG BRUISER: This large plastic tow truck was made by Marx in the sixties and is battery operated.

FLYING FOX: This all plastic, battery operated toy was made by Remco in the sixties. It features a realistic cockpit that allows you to raise, lower and steer the plane while the propellers spin.

SUZY HOMEMAKER ICE CREAM MAKER: This toy was made in 1968 by Topper Toys. This is only one of several Suzy Homemaker toys that came out in the sixties.

BIG LOO: This all plastic robot was made by Marx and measures 38" tall. He talks, has red flashing eyes, shoots darts, balls and grenades and also squirts water. He has a compass, sends morse code, whistles, rings a bell, has a scope, rolls on the floor and bends to pick up objects.

BARBIE HOT ROD: This all plastic hot rod was made in the early sixties. The hot rod is one of the Barbie vehicles that is fairly hard to find. This toy came with a red roll bar that is almost always missing. It was made for Mattel by Irwin Corp.

ARMY TRUCK AND CANNON: This big plastic truck and cannon were made by Ideal in the sixties. The truck features a removable canopy and a cannon that fires small cannon balls.

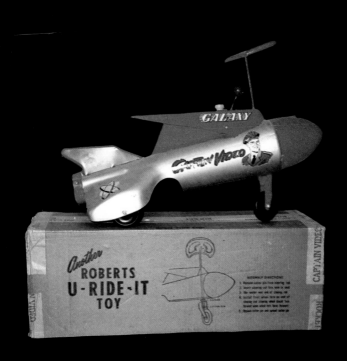

CAPTAIN VIDEO GALAXY RIDER: This toy was made in the fifties by Roberts. It was made for children to ride on.

SONAR SUB HUNT: This toy was made by Mattel in the sixties and is all plastic. This toy is very similar to the game Battleship, which later came out in a more advanced form called Electronic Battleship.

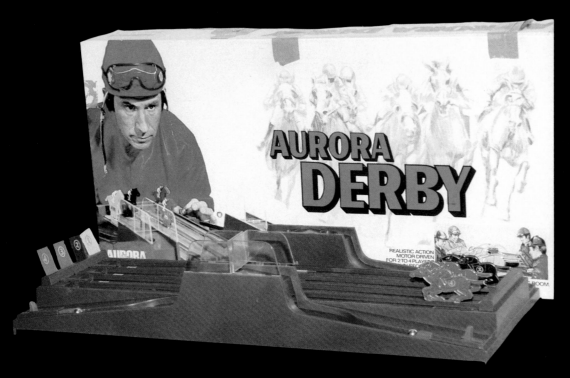

AURORA DERBY: This battery operated horse race game was made by Aurora in 1972. Don Adams is pictured on the toy box. He played in the series "Get Smart."

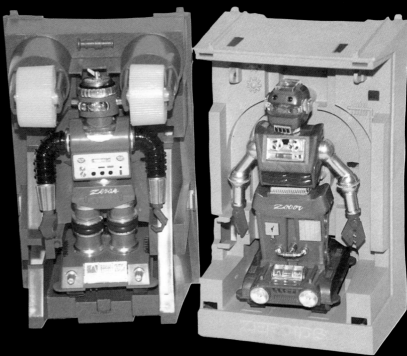

ROBOT HANDS: This all plastic toy was made by Kilgore in the fifties. It includes a face mask and plastic hands that can be worn.

ZEROIDS: Zeroids were made by Ideal in 1968 and were battery operated. They were sold individually and also in big boxed sets.

SHANGRI-LA CITY: This toy was made in 1969 by F. E. White Co., Inc. This is only one of three Shangri-la Cities produced. This is the deluxe set. The battery operated Sky Liner runs on a track through red rings and white stations.

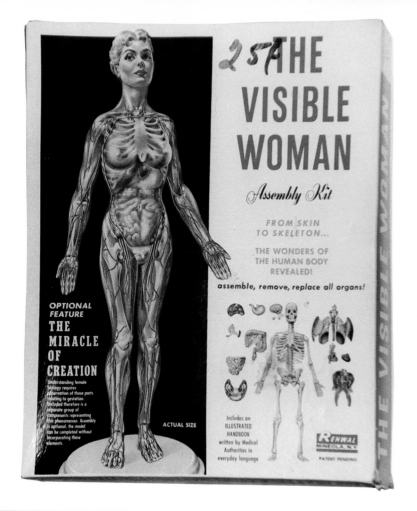

THE VISIBLE WOMAN: This plastic kit was made by Renwal in 1960. The kit came with optional parts that would show a woman in her seventh month of pregnancy. The optional parts were later removed from the kit due to protests.

BONANZA FIGURES: These plastic figures of Little Joe and his horse are part of a series of Bonanza figures that were produced by American Character in the sixties. The figures were sold separately. Each came with a horse and several accessories.

CHAPTER SIX
Nutty Mads, Weird-ohs and Rat Fink

In the early sixties toy manufacturers decided that children were ready for a change from the ordinary toys that were available. The alternative was a line of rather bizarre toys.

Louis Marx came out with Nutty Mads, Hawk Model Company produced Weird-ohs and Revell unveiled Rat Finks. The three lines of toys were very successful and these unusual toys played a large part in the memories of the children of the baby boom era.

The Marx Nutty Mad figures were injection molded poly plastic figures that averaged six inches in height. The Nutty Mads were not the only plastic figures that Marx made, but they were the most collectible of the plastic Marx figures. Marx produced Nutty Mads in several different shapes and forms. There were Nutty Mad cars, Nutty Mad tricycles and even a battery operated Nutty Mad Indian.

Weird-ohs were designed by Hawk Model Company and consisted of everything from model kits to magic slates. Hawk Model Company also produced plastic figures similar to the Marx Nutty Mads.

Rat Fink was designed by Ed "Big Daddy" Roth in 1963. Ed "Big Daddy" Roth worked for Revell designing Rat Fink model kits and Custom Monster kits. Ed's interest in custom cars initially attracted Revell. Ed's talents were used to design model kits featuring custom hot rods. Then came the Rat Fink and other bizarre creations combining hot rods with weird looking drivers. These proved to be a winning combination for Revell.

NUTTY GENERALS OR CARTOON SOLDIERS: These may be the rarest plastic figures ever made. They were made by Marx and very few are known to exist. Some of them were made in Great Britain. Pictured from left to right are, Flugel von Strudel (made in Great Britain), Igor the Mild (made in the U.S.A.) and Lt. Sake Sake (made in Great Britain). Not pictured are Col. Allistar McDuff, Manual Maracca, Sgt. Sweet and Eric Von Strudel.

NUTTY MADS: This bag contains a complete set of series one Nutty Mads, produced in the sixties by Marx. It is very uncommon to find an unopened set in the original package.

NUTTY MAD FIGURES SERIES 1: These hard plastic figures in Series 1 through 3 were made by Marx in the sixties. Pictured on the top row of Series 1 are Manny the Reckless Mariner (on the left), Waldo the Weight Lifter (center) and Donald the Demon (on the right). The bottom row includes Roddy the Hot Rod (left), Dippy the Deep Sea Diver (center) and Rocko the Champ (right).

NUTTY MAD FIGURES SERIES 2: Pictured on the top row are The Thinker (on the left), All Heart Hogan (center) and Suburban Sidney (on the right). Bottom row is Bull Pen Boo Boo (left), Chief Lost Teepee (center) and End Zone (right).

NUTTY MAD FIGURES SERIES 3: Pictured on the left is Hippo Crit, in the center is U.S. Male and on the right is Gutterball Annie.

NUTTY MAD FIGURES—SERIES 3: This third series is harder to find than series one and two. Pictured on the left is Now Children, in the center is Mudder and on the right is Smokey Sam.

NUTTY MAD CARS AND TRICYCLES: These Nutty Mad cars and tricycles were made by Marx in the sixties. The cars are friction powered and the tricycles are wind-ups.

NUTTY MAD INDIAN: This battery operated toy was made in the sixties by Marx. The Indian beats the drum while moving back and forth as he yells and sticks out his tongue. It measures 12" tall.

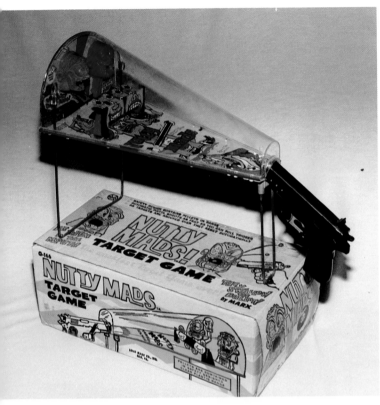

NUTTY MADS TARGET GAME: This part metal, part plastic target game was made in the sixties by Marx. This toy features knock down targets and a rapid firing pistol.

NUTTY MAD CAR AND BOAT/CAR: The Nutty Mad Car was made in the sixties by Marx and is battery operated. It measures 9¼" long and is mostly tin. The Nutty Mad Boat/Car is all plastic and was made in the sixties by Marx.

BLAME ITS: Blame Its were also made by Marx in the sixties and were much harder to find than the Nutty Mads series one and two. Pictured left to right are I Didn't Do It, I Didn't Push Him and I Didn't Paint It. Certain colors are hard to find. The light green is the most common color variation.

BLAME ITS: Pictured left to right are I Didn't Break It, I Didn't Eat It and I Didn't Get Dirty. These three colors are hard to find.

WEIRD-OHS MODEL KIT: Sling Rave Curvette, made by Hawk during the 1960s.

BLAME ITS: These light aqua colored Blame Its are the most common color variation. Pictured in the top photo are I Didn't Eat It (left), I Didn't Push Him (center) and I Didn't Break It (right). Pictured in the bottom photo are I Didn't Paint It (left), I Didn't Get Dirty (center) and I Didn't Do It (right).

WEIRD-OHS: These plastic figures were made in the sixties by Marx and licensed by Hawk Model Company Inc. in 1964. These are fairly hard to find. The common colors are red-orange and turquoise. Pictured in the top photo are Freddie Flameout (left), Daddy (center) and Digger (right). Pictured in the bottom photo are Davey (left), Drag Hag (center) and Endsville Eddie (right).

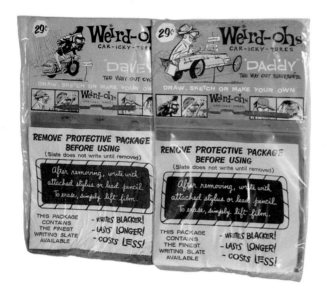

WEIRD-OHS "CAR-ICKY-TURES": These magic slates were made in the 1960s and licensed by Hawk Model Company.

DRAG HAG: This Weird-ohs model kit was made in the sixties by Hawk Model Company.

WEIRD-OHS GAME: The Weird-ohs board game was made in the sixties by Ideal and is highly sought after by both Weird-oh collectors and board game collectors.

MPC WEIRD-OHS: These plastic figures were made by MPC and are harder to find than the Hawk Weird-ohs or the third series Nutty Mads. Pictured left to right are Rockin' Ronnie, Beady Eye Bennie, Pin Head Pete and Fractured Francis. This is not the complete set. Missing in this photograph are Herculouse and Murry the Masher.

RAT FINKS: These small plastic Rat Finks were found in gum ball machines in the sixties. Some of them had holes in the back to snap on a plastic ring and others came with small chains.

THE SOUNDS OF THE WEIRD-OHS: This album was made in 1964 by Mercury Records and licensed by Hawk Model Co.

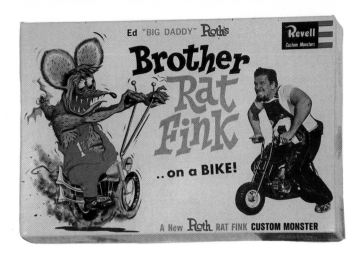

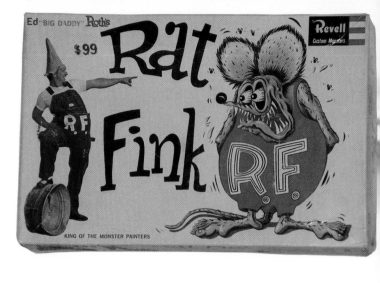

BROTHER RAT FINK ... ON A BIKE: This model kit was made in 1964 by Revell and was designed by Ed "Big Daddy" Roth.

RAT FINK: This model kit was made in 1963 by Revell and was designed by Ed "Big Daddy" Roth.

BORN LOSERS—"HITLER": This model kit was made in the 1960s by Parks. Parks only made three model kits and of the three model kits, the Born Losers "Hitler" kit is the most valuable. The other two kits are Born Losers "Napoleon" and Born Losers "Castro."

ANGEL FINK AND OUTLAW WITH ROBBIN HOOD FINK: These model kits were made in the sixties by Revell and were designed by Ed "Big Daddy" Roth.

MOTHER'S WORRY AND DRAG NUT: These model kits were made in the sixties by Revell. This line of Custom Monsters was designed by Ed "Big Daddy" Roth.

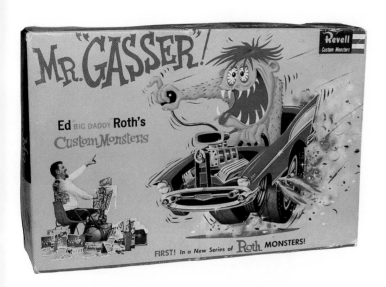

MR. GASSER: These model kits were made in the sixties by Revell and were designed by Ed "Big Daddy" Roth. The Mr. Gasser model kit pictured on bottom came equipped with a SP-500 motor.

TEDDY BALLOON BLOWING BEAR: Made in Japan in the fifties. The bear's eyes light and he kicks his feet as he blows up the balloon. Omits sound.

CHAPTER SEVEN
Battery Operated Toys

TEDDY THE ARTIST: This battery operated toy was made in Japan in the fifties. The bear closes his eyes and moves his head as he draws pictures. Nine different pictures can be made.

The battery operated toys of the fifties and sixties had clever actions and beautiful craftsmanship. The majority of collectors, however, will only buy these toys if they are in the original box. The box plays an important part in pricing battery operated toys, so the toys in this chapter will all be given a mint-in-the-box price.

Rare toys do not require a box to be valuable. The box will add to their value but rare toys will always be sought after by the collector, with or without a box.

When buying a battery operated toy it is important to know the actions the toy was made to perform. The toy box will usually have the toys' actions printed on the front or the side of the box. This is another reason collectors want the box.

Always look into the battery compartment when buying an old toy to see if there are any signs of corrosion. Batteries should never be left in the toy when it is stored. They can do corrosive damage in a short amount of time.

You may also look into the battery compartment to help determine the age of a toy. Toys from the fifties and sixties usually were made with metal battery compartments which were later replaced with plastic. The compartment also frequently had a battery painted on the inside, to show which way the battery should be inserted. Never be afraid to challenge the drawing in the battery compartment. Toys have been known to have the battery position drawings reversed from what they should be.

Most battery operated toys are repairable, but before buying a toy in need of work, be sure to check with a person who is knowledgeable in repairing old toys. Some toys are almost impossible to fix and others are not worth the price it would take to have them repaired.

ROYAL CUB: This toy was made in Japan. The bear pushes the carriage as the baby inside the carriage drinks a bottle while making crying noises.

COFFEETIME BEAR: This toy was made in Japan in the sixties. The bear pours coffee then drinks it. The coffee pot lights up and smokes.

PICNIC BEAR: Made in Japan in the 1950s. The bear pours the drink, drinks it, then the liquid circulates through the toy and appears in the bottle again. Eyes light up.

HUNGRY BABY BEAR: Made in Japan in the 1950s. The bear feeds her baby while her eyes open and close and the head moves. When the bottle is removed, the baby cries and kicks arms and legs.

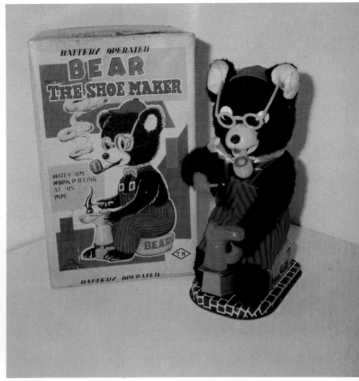

THE JOLLY PEANUT VENDOR: This toy was made in Japan for Cragstan in the fifties. The bear pushes the smoking cart as the peanuts move around. The cart has an interior light.

BEAR THE SHOE MAKER: Made in Japan in the 1960s. The bear hammers on the shoe while shaking his head and smoking his pipe.

POPCORN VENDOR: Made in Japan in the 1960s. The bear pedals the swaying cart while the umbrella spins and the popcorn pops.

SLEEPING BABY BEAR: Made in Japan in the 1950s. The alarm goes off and the bear sits up, stretches, closes his eyes and yawns.

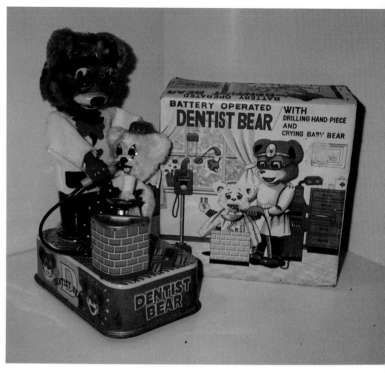

MOTHER BEAR: Made in Japan in the 1950s. The bear rocks as she knits.

DENTIST BEAR: Made in Japan in the 1950s. The dentist drills with a lighted drill, while moving head. The small bear moves his head and spits, while making a crying sound.

TELEPHONE BEAR: Made in Japan in the 1950s. The bear rocks, the phone rings and the bear holds receiver to ear while moving mouth and omitting sound.

TELEPHONE BEAR: Made in Japan in the 1950s. The bear writes, the phone rings and the bear speaks into the phone while nodding his head.

BLACKSMITH BEAR: Made in Japan in the 1950s. The bear hits the horseshoe with a hammer as his eyes light up. The anvil and forge also light up.

BEAR THE CASHIER: Made in Japan in the 1950s. The bear works the adding machine, then stops to answer the ringing phone.

SMOKING PAPA BEAR: Made in Japan in the 1950s, this toy operates by remote control. The bear walks along smoking a lighted pipe and exhaling the smoke.

SNEEZING BEAR: Made in Japan in the 1950s. The bear leans back and sneezes. Then he uses a tissue to wipe his nose. Eyes light up.

BARNEY BEAR THE DRUMMER BOY: Made in Japan in the 1950s. This toy operates by remote control. The bear walks along drumming with lighted eyes and turning head.

GRAND-PA PANDA BEAR: Made in Japan in the 1950s, the bear rocks with lighted eyes. Popcorn is brought to his mouth and he makes a chewing motion.

TEDDY BEAR SWING: Made in Japan in the 1950s, the bear flips over backward and forward on the swing.

SMOKING AND SHOE SHINING PANDA BEAR: Made in Japan in the 1950s, the bear shines his shoe, while smoking a lighted pipe.

MIGHTY MIKE: Made in Japan in the 1950s. The bear lifts the barbells over his head. The bear's eyes and the barbells both light up.

BLINKY THE CLOWN: Made in Japan in the 1950s. This remote control clown walks along with lighted eyes, moving head from side to side, while playing a drum.

BALL BLOWING CLOWN: Made in Japan in the 1950s. The clown's arms move and air is omitted from his mouth to keep a small ball suspended in air. The clown also features bump and go action.

CHARLIE THE DRUMMING CLOWN: Made in Japan in the 1950s. The clown's head moves and eyes light while playing the drums.

HAPPY THE CLOWN PUPPET SHOW: Made in Japan in the 1950s. The clown moves the puppet around while making different facial expressions.

CHARLIE THE FUNNY CLOWN: The clown rides along in a car with mop and pail in hands.

CLOWN THE MAGICIAN: Made in Japan in the 1950s. The clown tips his hat and does his magic trick with lighted nose and moving head.

DOZO THE STEAMING CLOWN: The clown was made in the sixties, sweeps with smoking broom, smoking hat and rolling eyes. When he bends over his pants smoke and he blushes.

JOLLY BAMBINO: Made in Japan in the 1950s. The candy rolls out of the can and the monkey eats it while kicking his legs and making a squeaking sound.

SUZETTE THE EATING MONKEY: Made in Japan in the 1950s. The monkey cuts up her food, places it in her mouth with a fork and goes through the motions of eating and swallowing it.

BONGO MONKEY: The monkey plays the bongos, moving back and forth, as his eyes light up. This toy was made in the sixties.

TRUMPET PLAYING MONKEY: Made in Japan in the 1950s, the monkey plays a trumpet and rings a bell with his foot while, at the same time, trying to swat a bee.

JOCKO THE DRINKING MONKEY: Made in Japan in the 1950s, the monkey pours liquid from a bottle and drinks it. The liquid circulates through the toy and comes back into the bottle. Jocko also features lighted eyes.

FRANKIE THE ROLLER SKATING MONKEY: Made in Japan in the 1950s, this toy is operated by remote control. The monkeys head, arms and legs all move as he roller skates.

CHIMPY THE JOLLY DRUMMER: The monkey plays the drums and cymbals with lighted eyes and moving head. The toy was made in the fifties.

BALLOON BLOWING MONKEY: The monkey's eyes light and he kicks his feet as he blows up the balloon. This toy also emits sound and was made in the fifties.

DANCING MERRY CHIMP: Buttons located on tin base will allow the monkey to clap, dance, move eyes, ears and mouth. The chimp was made in the sixties.

HY QUE MONKEY: This toy measures 17″ tall and is very difficult to repair when broken. The toy is activated by pressing a button in its palm. The monkey puts his hands over his mouth, his eyes and then his ears. He makes a chattering noise and smoke comes out of his ears. Hy Que Monkey was made in the sixties.

MISCHIEVOUS MONKEY: The monkey hangs onto the tree holding a bone until the dog sees him and comes out of his house to bark. This sends the monkey climbing back up the tree. This toy was made in the fifties.

PICNIC MONKEY: Made in the fifties, the monkey eats and drinks until his stomach appears to grow. Then he pats his stomach and makes a squeaking sound. When his stomach appears to return to normal, he begins to eat and drink again.

SPACE TRAVELING MONKEY: The monkey walks while carrying two suitcases. Periodically he puts the suitcases down and does a complete turnover.

BUBBLE BLOWING MONKEY: The monkey dips the wand into the soap solution, raises the wand to his mouth, holds his head back and blows bubbles. Features lighted eyes. This monkey was made in the fifties.

THE CHIMP AND PUP RAIL CAR: The two animals go up and down as the rail car rolls along. Both animals have lighted blinking eyes. This duo was made in the fifties.

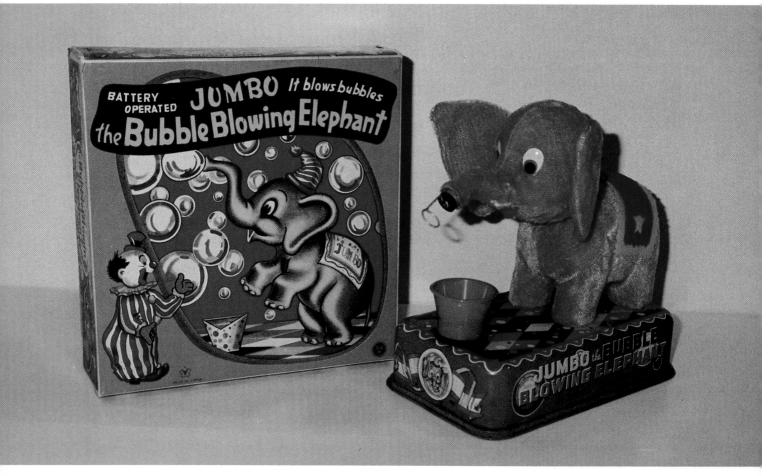

JUMBO THE BUBBLE BLOWING ELEPHANT: This toy has the same actions as the Bubble Blowing Monkey but the eyes do not light. Jumbo was made in the fifties.

BUBBLE BEAR: The bear has lighted eyes and moving arms and head. He lifts the lighted pipe to his mouth and blows bubbles. Bubble Bear was made in the fifties as well.

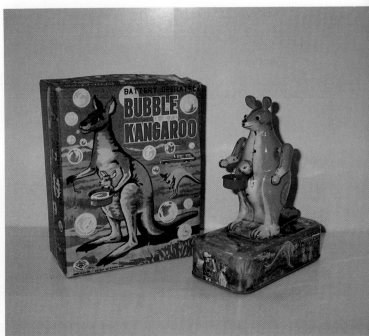

BUBBLE KANGAROO: Same action as Bubble Blowing Monkey but the eyes do not light. The kangaroo was also made in the fifties.

BUBBLE BLOWING BUNNY: This toy has the same actions as the Bubble Blowing Monkey but the eyes do not light. The bunny was also made in the fifties.

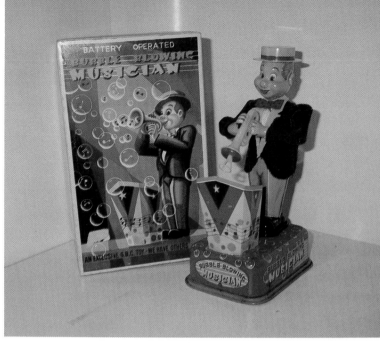

BUBBLE LION: The lion blows bubbles out his mouth. Features lighted eyes and moving head. Like the other bubble blowing animals, Bubble Lion was made in the fifties.

BUBBLE BLOWING MUSICIAN: The horn is dipped into the soap solution. Then he raises the horn to his mouth and blows bubbles. This toy was made in the fifties.

BUBBLE LOCOMOTIVE: The locomotive rolls along blowing bubbles out the smoke stack.

MR. MACPOOCH: This remote controlled dog walks along smoking a lighted pipe and exhaling the smoke. This toy was made in the fifties in Japan.

BURGER CHEF: Moving eyes and ears, the dog sways back and forth, salts and then flips the hamburger. Features a lighted cook top. Burger Chef was made in Japan in the 1950s.

FIDO: Fido was made in Japan in the fifties. The dog plays the xylophone with moving head and lighted eyes.

DANDY THE HAPPY DRUMMING PUP: Made in the fifties in Japan, the dog plays the drums and cymbals with moving head and eyes lit.

MUSICAL BULLDOG: The dog moves his arms up and down on the keyboard and the piano actually plays music. Features a smoking, lighted cigar. This toy was made in Japan in the fifties.

BUTTONS: The buttons located on the front of the toy, made in the sixties by Marx, allow Buttons to move paw, tail, eyes, head and mouth. Buttons also makes a barking sound.

PLAYFUL PUPPY WITH CATERPILLAR: The dog moves around barking at a moving caterpillar. It was made in the fifties in Japan. A similar version was made, called Playful Puppy With Mouse.

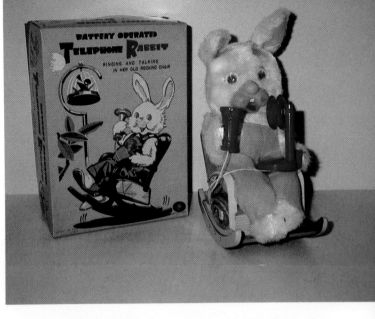

RABBIT AND CARRIAGE: The mother rabbit walks along pushing the carriage as the baby cries and lifts a carrot to his mouth. This toy was made in Japan in the fifties.

TELEPHONE RABBIT: The rabbit rocks, the phone rings and he answers it, moving his mouth and chattering. It was made in Japan in the fifties.

CAPPY THE BAGGAGE PORTER: The dog walks along with moving head and lighted eyes while pulling a cart. He stops, barks, then pulls the cart again. Cappy was made in Japan in the fifties.

PICNIC BUNNY: The rabbit pours a drink and drinks it. Then the liquid circulates through the toy and appears in the bottle again. Features lighted eyes. It was made in the fifties in Japan.

PETER THE DRUMMING RABBIT: This toy operates by remote control. The rabbit walks with moving head and lighted eyes while playing the drum. It was made in Japan in the fifties.

GRASSHOPPER: The grasshopper runs along making a chirping noise. Features non-stop action.

TALKING PARROT: This toy measures 18″ tall and was made in Japan in the fifties. It contains a tape recorder that will record and play back everything you say. The bird turns his head, flaps his wings and tail and has lighted eyes.

DRINKING LICKING CAT: The cat pours milk in the cup and uses her tongue to drink it with a licking motion. Features lighted eyes.

DENNIS THE MENACE: As Dennis plays "London Bridge" on the xylophone, his head and arms move back and forth. Dennis was made in Japan in the fifties.

OL' SLEEPY HEAD RIP: A chirping, spinning bird wakes up Rip Van Winkle. He sits up with lighted face, stretches, yawns, and lies back down. Rip was made in Japan in the fifties.

FEEDING BIRD WATCHER: Made in the fifties by Linemar, the mother bird flies off the branch to the nest of chirping baby birds. The babies open their mouths and the mother feeds them a worm.

TWO GUN SHERIFF: This remote control toy features moving eyes, a chewing motion and firing guns that make a rat-tat-tat noise.

MAJOR TOOTY: The drum major beats the drums in a marching rhythm and blows a whistle. This toy was made in the sixties in Japan.

116

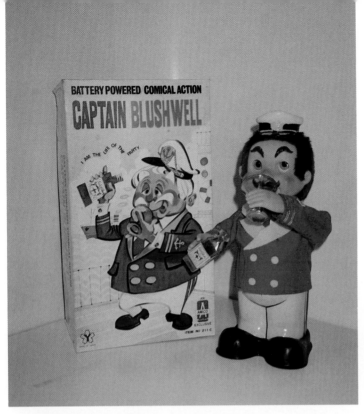

CAPTAIN BLUSHWELL: The captain pours a drink and drinks it. Then his face lights up and his eyes begin to spin. He was made in Japan in the 1960s.

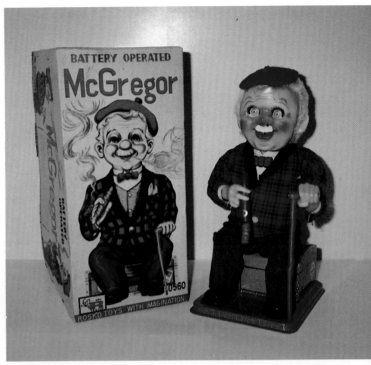

MCGREGOR: Made in the sixties in Japan, McGregor smokes a lighted cigar, blows smoke from his mouth, opens and closes his eyes, stands up and sits down.

DRINKING CAPTAIN: The Captain takes a drink, his stomach lights up and then begins to smoke. Features a lighted post and eyes that open and close. This toy was made in the sixties in Japan.

GOOD TIME CHARLIE: Charlie sits on a trash can drinking his drink, smoking his cigar and kicking his foot with a lighted face. Features a lighted street lamp. Charlie was made in Japan in the sixties.

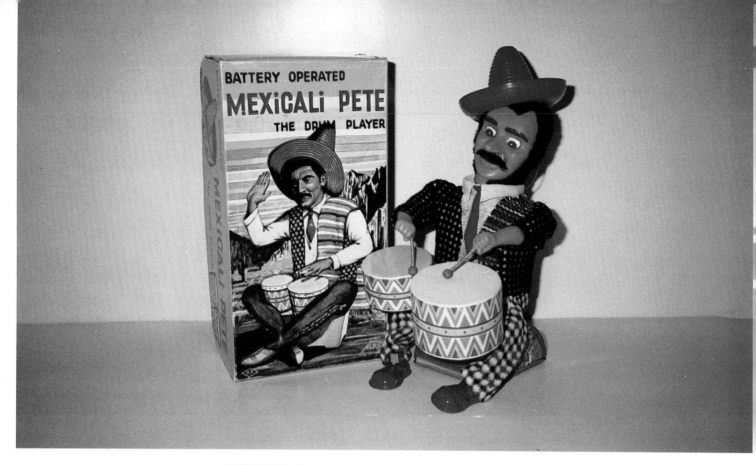

MEXICALI PETE: Pete plays the drum while moving his body from side to side. He was made in Japan in the sixties.

SAM THE SHAVING MAN: Made in Japan in the sixties, Sam's face lights up as he shaves. When finished, he looks in the mirror and powders his face.

SWITCHBOARD OPERATOR: Made in the fifties by Linemar, this is one of several Dolly toys that were made. This model is harder to find than the others. The girl operates the lighted switchboard, moving her head and arms.

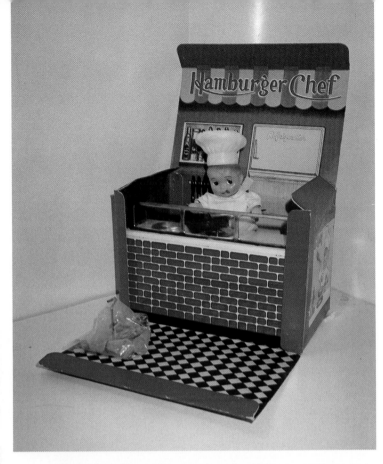

HAMBURGER CHEF: The Chef holds a frying pan and cooks over a lighted grill, using the spatula for turning. He was made in Japan in the sixties.

STRUTTING MY FAIR DANCER: Made in Japan in the fifties, the girl dances around, moving her arms and legs in all directions.

CLIMBING LINESMAN: The man shimmies up and down the pole that extends from the work truck. Features working head lamp. This linesman was made in Japan in the fifties.

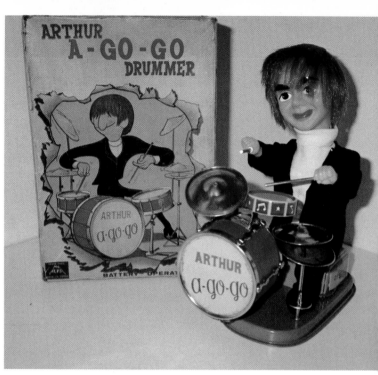

SMOKING GRANDPA: The man rocks in the rocking chair, smoking the lighted pipe and exhaling the smoke. There are two versions of this toy. The version with closed eyes is the most valuable. Grandpa was made in the fifties in Japan.

PUFFY MORRIS: This toy actually smokes a cigarette when inserted in the cigarette holder. His eyes and chest move. Puffy was made in the sixties in Japan.

ARTHUR A-GO-GO DRUMMER: Made in Japan in the 1960s, Arthur plays the drums and cymbals while moving head from side to side.

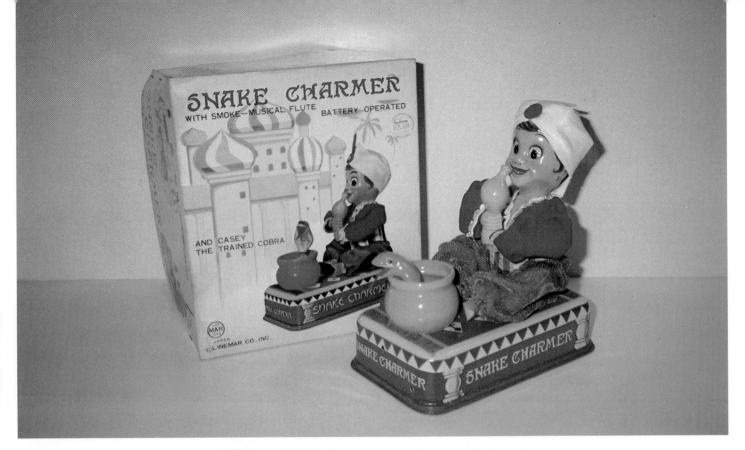

SNAKE CHARMER: The man plays a musical flute and a snake appears with smoke coming out of the basket. This toy was made in the fifties by Linemar.

WESTERN BAD MAN: The cowboy drinks the beer, his face lights up and he shoots his gun as the bartender ducks. He was made in the sixties in Japan.

MR. BASEBALL JR.: The ball player hits the ball each time the automatic batting machine has one ready. He was made in the fifties in Japan.

ROULETTE "A GAMBLING MAN": Made in the sixties by Cragstan, the wheel turns and the man makes facial expressions as he places the marble on the wheel.

PINOCCHIO: Pinocchio was made in Japan in the sixties. He plays "London Bridge" on the xylophone as he moves his head and arms.

INDIAN JOE: The Indian, made in the sixties in Japan, plays the drum, moving his head from side to side.
Chapter 7/92 37-08

TRAFFIC POLICEMAN: Made in the sixties in Japan, the policeman blows his whistle and waves his arms to stop traffic. As the light changes, he starts the traffic moving again.

HAPPY SANTA: Made in the fifties in Japan, Santa plays the drums and cymbals while moving his head from side to side. This toy has lighted eyes, but there is another version that does not have lighted eyes.

SANTA CLAUS: Santa rings the bell with swaying body, lighted eyes and turning head.

SANTA ON ROTATING GLOBE: Santa rings the bell, moving his head and arms while sitting on a rotating globe.

SANTA ON SCOOTER AND SPACE SCOOTER: Both toys feature head and tail lights and bump and go action. The Santa toy makes a bell sound. The space toy has a realistic engine noise. Both toys were made in Japan in the sixties.

KISSING COUPLE: Made in Japan in the fifties, this bump and go car features a chirping celluloid bird. The couple turn and kiss and the man's face lights up with embarrassment.

SPACE PATROL: This bump and go vehicle measures 11" long and was made in Japan in the sixties. Features moving TV camera and flashing booster light.

FIRE CHIEF CAR: This toy measures 9 ¾" long and was made in the sixties in Japan. Features ringing bell, mystery action and automatic steering.

TURN-O-MATIC GUN JEEP: This toy measures 10" long and was made in Japan in the sixties. Features mystery action, working light and a gun that pops out of the hood.

HIGHWAY PATROL: This toy was made in the sixties and measures 11 ¾" long. It features stop and go action, working headlight and a policeman who actually gets on and off the motorcycle.

FIRE CHIEF CAR NO. 7: This toy features mystery action, blinking light and siren.

FIRE TRICYCLE: This toy was made in Japan in the sixties. It features working headlight, mystery action and automatic steering.

POLICE PATROL JEEP: This toy features working light, automatic steering and mystery action.

BATTLE HELICOPTER: This toy was made in Japan in the early seventies. It has two plastic propellers that stop automatically as the helicopter stops rolling, then they begin revolving as the toy automatically starts to roll again.

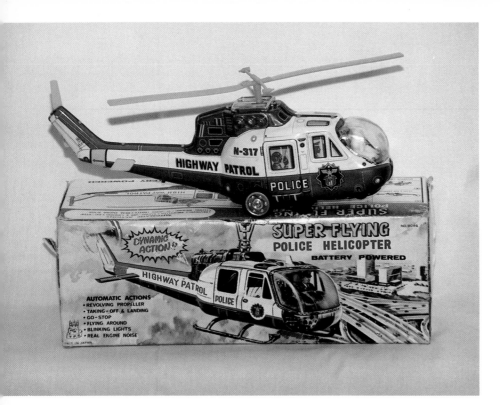

SUPER FLYING POLICE HELI-
COPTER: This toy was made in the
sixties in Japan. It features blinking
lights, engine noise and revolving
propeller. It actually lifts up off the
ground as well.

WHISTLING SHOW BOAT: This toy
was made in the fifties and measures
14″ long. It features smoking stack
and a whistling noise. It also automatically changes directions.

DOUGLAS DC-9 JET PLANE: This toy features stop and go action, lighted engines with noise and a small door that opens to reveal stairs with a stewardess at the top.

MULTI-ACTION ELECTRA JET: This toy measures 14" long, has a 17" wing span and was made in the sixties in Japan. Features stop and go action, turning propellers and working lights.

AUTOMATIC TAKE-OFF AND LANDING JET: This American Airlines jet has blinking lights and features automatic take off and landing.

BOEING 747 JET PLANE: This toy was made in the seventies. It features lighted engines and engine noise.

PAN AM BOEING 747 JUMBO JET: This toy was made in Japan in the early seventies. It features stop and go action, plastic see through cockpit, lighted engines and engine noise.

CHAPTER EIGHT
Race Cars

Race cars are almost always a sound investment. Look for rubber tires and cars that feature famous racing teams. The gas powered thimble dromes are always good investments. The thimble dromes that are part plastic are less valuable then the all metal cars.

When investing in race cars, always remember to consider the condition. Whether it is race cars or any other toy, the condition is always one of the most important things to look for. Never buy a toy that is not in excellent to near mint condition and whenever possible, try to purchase toys that are mint-in-the-box.

PORSCHE CARRERA RALLY: This battery operated car was made in Japan in the sixties. It measures 10½" long and features bump 'n go action.

FIREBIRD SPEEDWAY RACER: This friction car was made by Cragstan in the sixties and measures 15" long. It features engine noise and removable inflatable tires.

JET RACER: This friction car was made in Japan in the fifties and measures 8½″ long. The car makes noise when the wheels turn.

PORSCHE RACER: This battery operated car was made in Japan. It features bump 'n go action with engine sound.

PORSCHE 917K: This battery operated car was made by Sears in the seventies. It features non-fall and bump 'n go action.

VW PORSCHE 914: This battery operated car was made in Japan in the late sixties. It features non-stop action.

DISTLER PORSCHE: This battery operated car was made in Germany in the fifties. It measures 10½" long, features a steering wheel that actually turns the wheels and a gear shift that shifts from first to second, into reverse or neutral.

COMET RACER: This friction car was made in Japan in the sixties and measures 9″ long.

Three photos:

JET RACER: This friction car was made in Japan in the late sixties. It measures 10″ long.

MERCEDES RACER: This battery operated car was made in West Germany in the sixties. It measures 9½" long.

INTERNATIONAL STOCK RACE CAR: This friction car was made in Japan in the late sixties. This car was part of a series of race cars that were made to represent different countries.

FERRARI 250/LEMANS: This battery operated car was made in Japan in the late sixties.

FERRARI 365GT BB: This battery operated car was made in Japan in the late sixties. It features non-fall and bump 'n go action.

LAMBORGHINI COUNTACH: This battery operated car was made in Japan in the sixties. It features non-fall and bump 'n go action.

CHAPARRAL 2F: This battery operated car was made in Japan in the sixties. It features stop and go action, moving air-foil, steerable front wheels and flashing head lights.

FIRESTONE RACE CAR: This wind-up plastic race car was sold by Firestone. The car is a scale model of the one driven by race car driver Rex Mays.

BMW 3.5 CSL TURBO: This battery operated car was made in Japan in the sixties. It features non-fall and bump 'n go action.

RALLYE RACE CAR SET: This wind-up race car set was made in Germany by Technofix. It was made in the fifties. It came with four tin cars and a plastic track.

STUNT CAR: This battery operated car was made in Japan in the sixties. The car is tin and the drivers head is vinyl. It runs in a circle making body outside up and has realistic sound.

CHAMPION MIDGET RACER: This friction car was made in Japan in the fifties.

ROCKET CAR: This friction car was made in Japan in the fifties. When rolled, this car emits sparks.

PORSCHE: This battery operated car was made in Japan in the fifties and measures 11½" long.

MERCEDES RACER: This wind-up car was made in West Germany and measures 10½" long.

CORVETTE: This battery operated car was made in Japan in the late sixties. It features non-fall, bump 'n go action and measures 10" long.

RACE CAR: This all tin friction car was made in Japan in the fifties and measures 5" long.

PORSCHE 911 S SAFARI RALLY: This battery operated car was made in Japan in the late sixties and features mystery action, blinking light and engine noise.

BIG STUNT CAR: This battery operated toy was made in Japan in 1969. This Mach 1 Mustang will go forward, turn over, incline, then go forward again.

GO STOP BENZ RACER: This battery operated Mercedes racer was made in Japan in the fifties. It features stop and go action and working lights.

FORD G.T. 40: This battery operated toy was made in Japan in the 1960s for Sears. It features spin-out action and running movement.

CHAPTER NINE
Hanna-Barbera

To say that Bill Hanna and Joe Barbera created world famous cartoons is an understatement. From 1940 to 1957 Bill Hanna and Joe Barbera worked together creating cartoons for M.G.M. When M.G.M. closed their cartoon division in 1957 Hanna and Barbera began working together, independent of any major studio. Shortly thereafter they created their first short, Ruff and Ready.

This was the beginning for Hanna-Barbera Studio's. In the fall of 1960, the Hanna-Barbera Studio's produced the first animated series to be seen on prime time television. It was called "The Flintstones."

"The Flintstones" was to be Hanna-Barbera's most popular creation, airing 166 episode. Huckleberry hound, created in 1958, this was the first animated cartoon to receive an Emmy for "Outstanding Achievement In Childrens Programming."

Other Hanna Barbera creations included some less celebrated but equally familiar names. "Pixie and Dixie" was first shown in 1958, "Quick Draw McGraw" was introduced in 1959, "Yogi Bear" was created in 1960 and "Top Cat" was first shown in 1961. Top Cat is known as "Boss Cat" in England.

Finally, "The Jetsons" first aired in September of 1962. "The Jetsons" originally aired on Sunday nights, but because of competition from "The Wonderful World of Disney" and "Dennis the Menace," which were also on at the same time, the ratings were not good. After changing the show to Saturday mornings, the ratings went through the roof.

The end results of Bill Hanna and Joe Barbera's creations were far more than could be measured. They created the laughter of a child and the fond memories of a grownup. Having grown up, looking back at Fred Flintstone one does not simply see a cartoon character but an old friend. Fred Flintstone represents all the good things of our childhood.

Baby Boomers will always associate Hanna-Barbera cartoons with good times, laughter and excitement. Seeing an old Hanna-Barbera cartoon will always put a smile on the face of a Baby Boomer.

TV-TINYKINS: These small plastic hand painted figures were made by Marx in 1961. This set is called the gift box.

FLINTSTONE TINYKINS: These plastic hand painted figures were made by Marx in the sixties.

TV-TINYKINS: These small hand painted plastic figures were made by Marx in the sixties. Yogi Bear cartoon characters are on the top shelf and Quick Draw McGraw cartoon characters are on the bottom.

TV-TINYKINS: These small hand painted plastic figures were made by Marx in the sixties. Top shelf features Top Cat characters, bottom shelf features Huckleberry Hound characters.

TV PLAY SET AND TV SCENES: Thses small plastic figures were made by Marx in the sixties. Each box features a colorful background. Toy on top is Yogi bear. Second shelf is Top Cat on left, Yogi Bear center and Flintstones are on the right.

TOM AND JERRY LOCOMOTIVE: This toy was made in the sixties and is battery operated. It has bump and go action, the lantern lights up and it makes loud train noises.

TOM AND JERRY HAND CAR: This battery operated toy was made in Japan in the sixties. It has bump and go action and emits sound, as Jerry pumps the handcar.

FLINTSTONE DAKINS: These vinyl figures were made by Dakin in the seventies.

FRED FLINTSTONE AND BAMM BAMM: These squeak toys were made in Spain in the sixties by Lanco. Fred is on the left and Bamm Bamm is on the right.

FLINTSTONE TRUCK: This friction toy was made by Linemar in the sixties. This is one of the Flintstone toys that is hard to find.

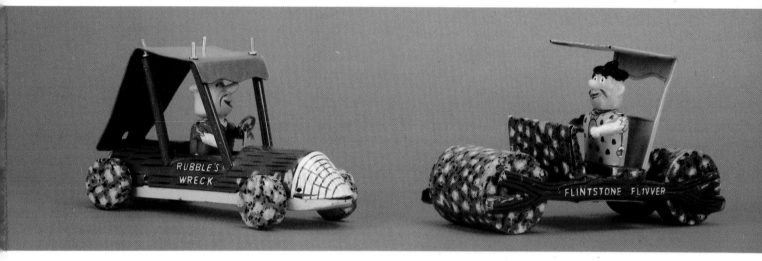

RUBBLE'S WRECK AND FLINTSTONE FLIVVER: These two toys were made in the sixties by Marx. The Rubble's Wreck is a battery operated toy and the Flintstone Flivver is a friction toy.

FLINTSTONE CARS: These toys were made by Marx in the sixties and are operated by friction. They all came in the same type of box. The box says Huckleberry Car on the front.

FLINTSTONE CAR: This battery operated, all plastic toy
was made in Hong Kong in 1974.

FLINTSTONE BEDROCK EXPRESS: This tin wind-up toy was made in the sixties by Marx. It rolls along in a zig-zag motion.

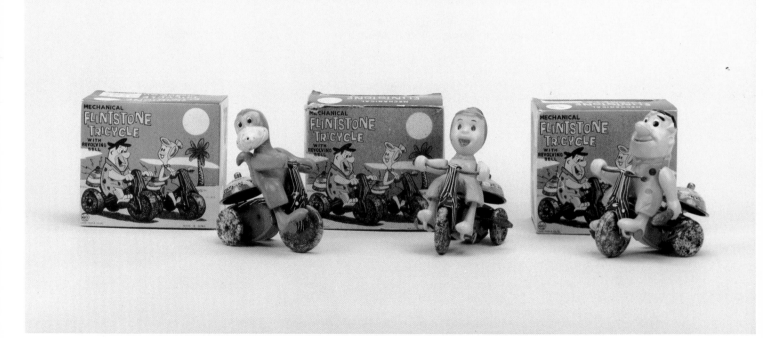

FLINTSTONE TRICYCLE: These wind-up toys were made in the sixties by Marx. The boxes were all the same, but the names were changed on the side of each box.

FRED FLINTSTONE ON DINO: This battery operated toy
was made in the sixties by Marx. Dino walks, moves tail,
neck and mouth, while whistling.

FRED FLINTSTONE ON DINO AND FLINTSTONE PALS: These tin wind-up toys were made in the sixties by Marx. Fred is on the left and Barney is on the right.

DINO-THE-DINOSAUR: This tin wind-up toy was made by Linemar in the sixties. When wound up, Dino walks and growls.

HOPPING FRED FLINTSTONE AND BARNEY RUBBLE: These two wind-up toys were made by Marx in the sixties. When wound they hop up and down. On the left is Fred and on the right is Barney.

FLINTSTONE TURNOVER TANK: This tin wind-up toy was made by Linemar in the sixties. This toy featured two different arrangements of characters. Fred picks up the rank and rolls it over.

SLANT WALKERS: These plastic toys were made in the sixties by Marx. Featured on the left are Fred and Wilma, on the right is Pebbles.

HANNA-BARBERA PUSH UP PUPPETS: Featured left to right are Fred Flintstone, Wilma, Dino, Pebbles and Bamm Bamm.

FRED FLINTSTONE'S BEDROCK BAND: This battery operated toy was made in Japan in the sixties. Fred plays the drums and cymbals.

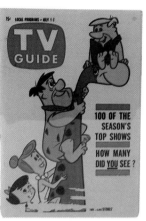

SPINIKIN: These plastic toys were made in the sixties by Kohner Bros. Inc. The plastic figure spins around when the ring is pulled.

TV GUIDES: The one on the left came out on July 1, 1961. The TV Guide on the right came out on June 13, 1964. Both feature the Flintstones on the cover.

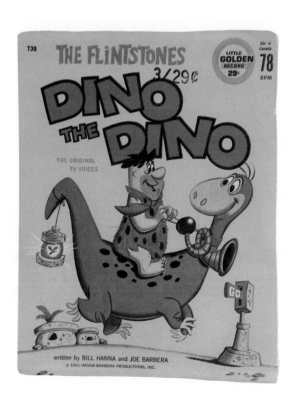

FLINTSTONES RECORD: This Dino the Dino record was made in 1963 by Little Golden Record. Words were written by Bill Hanna and Joe Barbera.

PEBBLES AND BAMM-BAMM PAPER DOLLS: These paper dolls were made by Whitman in 1966 and licensed by Hanna-Barbera.

ROCKY: This battery operated toy was made in Japan in the sixties. This toy was made to look like Fred Flintstone, but was unlicensed by Hanna-Barbera.

PIXIE AND DIXIE CERAMIC FIGURE: This was made for Idea's Inc. but never mass produced. It is possibly a prototype piece.

FRED FLINTSTONE AND HUCKLEBERRY HOUND PULL TOYS: These wooden toys were made by Fisher Price in the sixties. When you pull them across the floor by their cords, they play their xylophones.

HANNA-BARBERA CERAMIC FIGURES: These ceramic figures were made in the sixties by Idea's Inc. Pictured left to right: Yogi Bear, Huckleberry Hound, Mr. Jinx, Quick Draw McGraw and Baba Loo.

YOGI BEAR: This stuffed Yogi Bear was made by Ideal in 1962.

QUICK DRAW MCGRAW AND HUCKLEBERRY HOUND
WALL PLAQUES: These hard plastic wall plaques were
made in the early seventies and they measure 11" tall.

QUICK DRAW MCGRAW: This stuffed Quick Draw
McGraw was made by Ideal in 1962.

TOUCHE TURTLE: This stuffed Touche Turtle was made
in 1962 by Ideal.

MAGILLA GORILLA: The toy on the left was made in 1964 by Ideal and measures 8″ tall. It may be posed in different positions. The toy on the right is a stuffed toy that was made in the sixties.

HANNA BARBERA SQUEAK TOYS: These squeak toys were made in Spain in the sixties by Lanco. Top row: Magilla Gorilla, Huckleberry Hound and Top Cat. Bottom row: Boo Boo, Yogi Bear and two Jerry figures.

MAGILLA GORILLA: This stuffed toy was made by Playtime Toys in the seventies.

HUCKLEBERRY HOUND: This squeak toy was made in the sixties by Dell. It measures 6″ tall.

MAGILLA GORILLA: This soft rubber toy was made in
Spain in the sixties by Lanco.

YOGI BEAR AND HUCKLEBERRY HOUND SQUEAK TOYS: These soft rubber squeak toys were made in Spain in the sixties by Lanco.

YOGI BEAR SQUEAK TOY: This soft rubber squeak toy was made in Spain in the sixties by Lanco.

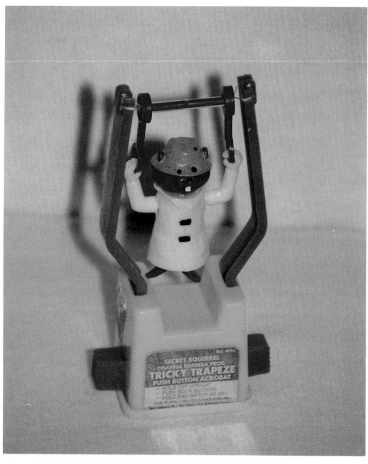

SECRET SQUIRREL TRICKY TRAPEZE: This toy was made in Hong Kong in 1967 for Kohner Bros. There are several different versions of this toy. This Secret Squirrel version is harder to find than most.

HANNA-BARBERA PUSH UP PUPPETS: These plastic toys were made in the sixties by Kohner Bros. Inc. When you press upward on the base, the figure moves. *Left to right:* Magilla Gorilla, Touche Turtle, Wally Gator, Secret Squirrel, Ricochet Rabbit and Huckleberry Hound.

HUCKLEBERRY GO-MOBILES: These friction toys were made in the sixties and they all came with the same card. Pictured on the left is Quick Draw McGraw, on the right is Yogi Bear. This toy was also made featuring Huckleberry Hound.

HUCKLEBERRY CARS: These friction toys were made in the sixties by Marx. Pictured on the left is Yogi Bear, center is Huckleberry Hound and on the right is Quick Draw McGraw. The boxes were the same for each toy.

ANIMAL AIRPLANE: This friction toy was made by Linemar in the sixties. It was also made featuring Yogi Bear and Quick Draw McGraw.

HANNA-BARBERA HOPPING TOYS: These tin wind-up toys were made in the sixties by Marx. When wound up they hop around in a circle. Pictured on the left is Quick Draw McGraw, center is Huckleberry Hound, right is Yogi Bear.

SLANT WALKERS: These plastic toys were made in the sixties by Marx. They walk when placed in a slanting position. Featured on the left are Yogi and Huckleberry Hound, center is Top Cat and Benny, on the right is Fred Flintstone and Barney Rubble.

YOGI BEAR AND CINDY PUSH BUTTON PUPPETS: These plastic toys were made by Kohner Bros. Inc. in the sixties. The figures move when you push up the base.

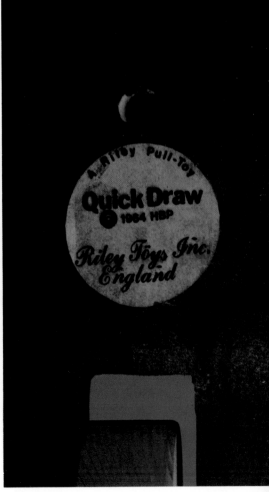

QUICK DRAW PULL TOY: This wooden pull toy was passed off as a rare toy made in 1964, but it was actually hand made recently by a con artist. The dated manufacturers label was also produced to fool collectors. Beware, several are known to exist.

JETSON HOPPING TOYS: These tin wind-up toys were made in the sixties by Marx. This shows the complete set. Pictured from left to right are Rosie, Astro, George and Elroy. They have the same action as the Flintstone hoppers.

JETSON EXPRESS: This tin wind-up train was made in the sixties by Marx. It rolls along in a zig-zag motion.

JETSONS TURNOVER TANK: This tin wind-up toy was made by Linemar in the sixties. George picks up the tank and rolls it over.

SCOOBY DOO SQUEAK TOY: This soft rubber squeak toy was made in Spain in the early seventies by Lanco.

SPIKE SQUEAK TOY: This soft rubber squeak toy was made in Spain in the sixties by Lanco.

JETSON SLANT WALKERS: These all plastic toys were made in the sixties by Marx. They walk when placed in a slanting position.

HAIR BEARS: These Hair Bears squeak toys were made in Spain in the early seventies by Dolax.

HAIR BEAR: This plush Hair Bear was made in the seventies by Sutton.

CHAPTER TEN
Wind-up Toys

HAPPY LIFE: Made in Japan in the 1950s, this celluloid and tin wind-up toy features a girl that rocks back and forth under a spinning umbrella as the duck goes around. This same toy came out in the 1930s, but this later version is much more detailed.

ROCKING DOG WITH WHIRLING ROPE: This all tin wind-up toy was made in Japan in the 1950s. The dog rocks back and forth as a lasso twirls overhead.

SKIP ROPE ANIMALS: Made in the 1950s, the small bear jumps rope as the chipmunk moves back and forth. This all tin windup toy is a TPS Japan toy.

BOUNCING DOLLY BALL AND SUZY BOUNCING BALL: Bouncing Dolly Ball was made in Japan in the 1950s and this wind-up toy is all tin except for the head, which is vinyl. Suzy Bouncing Ball was also made in Japan in the 1950s and is all tin except for the head and the cloth skirt, which is usually missing. Several versions of this pony tailed girl were produced, one as a typist, one riding a bicycle and one that sews on a sewing machine.

SEA WOLF: This primarily tin, partly plastic, windup toy was made in Japan in the 1960s. The pirate vibrates around in a circle, then raises the telescope to one eye as the other eye closes.

MONKEY CAROUSAL: This wind-up toy was made in Japan in the 1960s and measures 6½" tall. The monkeys go around in a ferris wheel manner, while a bell rings. An on and off switch is located under the bell.

VACATION LAND AIRPLANE RIDE: Made in Japan in the 1960s, this wind-up toy has an on and off switch. As the airplanes fly around the tower, the boats circle beneath the tower.

TOM TOM JUNGLE BOY: This wind-up toy was made by
Marx in the 1950s and is mostly tin.

SQUIRREL LAND: This wind-up toy was made in Japan in the 1950s and when wound up, the squirrel goes down the trail, circles and comes back again, spinning the colorful spinner each time he passes by.

ROLLERSKATING CLOWN: This wind-up toy was made by Linemar in the 1950s. The clown skates, pushing off with his right foot, while the head and arms remain stationary. This toy also appeared as a white faced clown, which is a lot less common than this bearded version.

CUBBY THE READING BEAR: This wind-up toy was made in Japan in the 1960s and is made of fur, cloth and tin. The book pages are all metal and the bear turns the pages with a magnet that is attached to his paw.

SKIPPY THE TRICKY CYCLIST: This wind-up toy was made in Japan in the 1950s and features an all tin clown wearing cloth clothes. When wound, he rolls along while trying to stay balanced on the unicycle.

LITTLE MONKEY SHINER: This part tin, part fur wind-up toy was made in Japan in the 1960s and measures 6½" tall. As he buffs the boot, his head and boot both turn. This is only one of several monkey wind-ups that were made by T.N. of Japan. Other similar versions include Little Monkey Shoe Maker, Make-up Monkey, Monkey Bartender and Monkey Machine Gun.

MILTON BERLE CAR: This wind-up car was made in the 1950s by Marx and operates much like the Marx Whoopee cars that were made in the late twenties. The car spins around in circles with crazy car action.

DONKEY BOY: This tin wind-up toy was made in Japan in the 1960s and features a boy riding a bucking donkey.

MECHANICAL FUR MONKEY ON CYCLE: This wind-up toy was made in Japan in the sixties. The monkey's body is made of cardboard and covered in fur. The hands and face are plastic and when wound, the monkey balances, moving back and forth on a tin wheel.

CASEY JR.—THE DISNEYLAND EXPRESS: This wind-up train was made by Marx in the fifties. The engine is plastic and the cars are tin with Disney characters featured on each car.

CIRCUS PARADE: This wind-up toy was made in Japan in the 1950s. The elephant rolls forward as the clowns go 'round and 'round.

HAPPY GRAND'PA: Made in Japan in the 1960s, this wind-up toy has a bell that rings as the chickens peck the ground, the umbrella spins around and grand'pa rocks back and forth.

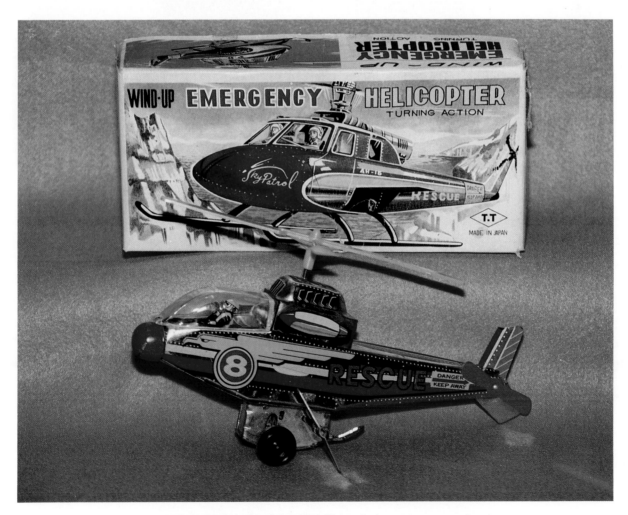

EMERGENCY HELICOPTER: This wind-up toy was made in Japan in the 1960s and features a plastic propeller that revolves as the toy rolls along.

BICYCLE WIND-UP: This toy was made in Japan in the fifties. The head is vinyl.

DISNEY WHIRLIGIG: This toy is unmarked. It is made of celluloid and plastic, with a vinyl bee. The toy features Disney characters, but is unlicensed by Disney.

COMIC HELICOPTER: This helicopter was made in the sixties. The nose is vinyl and the small propeller is plastic.

FLAPPING BUTTERFLY: This wind-up toy was made in
Japan in the sixties. The butterfly flaps his wings then
pauses and flutters them.

GRAND-PA'S NEW CAR: This all tin wind-up toy was
made in Japan in the fifties. The car rolls around in a
circle as Grandpa rocks back and forth.

Top left: Rare Beatles book binder. Made in U.K. in 1964. This grey cloth binder measures 9"x6½" and was made to hold twelve issues of Beatles magazines. *Top center:* 6" Beatles bowl, made in U.K. by Washington pottery. *Top center:* Beatles Yellow Submarine, made in 1968 by Corgi. *Top right:* Plastic tumbler and plastic mug. Both were made in 1964 by Burrite. Tumbler measures 6¼" tall and mug measures 4" tall. *Bottom left:* Beatles bubble bath containers, made in 1964 by Colgate-Palmolive. They measure 9" tall. *Bottom center:* Beatles dolls by Remco. They measure 5" tall and were made in 1964. *Bottom front:* Harmonica, made by Hohner, measuring 5" long.

CHAPTER ELEVEN
The Beatles

There is very little that can be said about "The Beatles" that has not already been said. It would be impossible, however, to discuss the Baby Boom era without mentioning "The Beatles."

Children, teenagers and even parents of the sixties were all familiar with this rock group from Liverpool, England. "The Beatles" gained worldwide recognition in a very short time. Teenagers began to form fan clubs. Promoters were busy producing every type of Beatles souvenir imaginable. "Beatlemania" quickly spread across America and almost every product that promoted "The Beatles" was quickly bought by fans who began collecting Beatles items.

Some of the items that have become almost impossible to find by today's Beatles collectors are the items that were used in the sixties and then discarded. Beatles hair spray, perfume and talcum powder are a few of these hard to find items. In 1990, a cereal box featuring an advertisement on the back for *Yellow Submarine* turned up and was auctioned off for over $700. This box was dated 1969 and happened to be one that the collectors were unfamiliar with. Auctions are known to have unrealistic prices and this price is probably a good example.

"The Beatles" popularity continued through the entire decade of the sixties and, over the years, Beatles items have become ever more collectible.

BEATLE COLLECTIBLES: *Left to right: Yellow Submarine* alarm clock, made in 1968 by Sheffield Watch Inc., rubber coated, insulated glass, 5½" tall, made in 1964; Talcum Powder made by Margo of Mayfair in 1964 and measures 7" tall; Perfume Bottle made in 1964 by Olive Adair Co., Liverpool, England; Beatle Hair Spray made in 1964 by Bonsor Products; Rare *Yellow Submarine* Candle made by Concept Development in 1968.

BEATLES PERFUME: This is possibly the rarest of all the Beatle items. This perfume was made in Liverpool, England and introduced to Beatle fans in early 1964.

BEATLES BAGS AND CASES: *Top left:* Overnight bag, made by Airflite. It came in black or red vinyl and featured zipper opening. It's 13″ tall and made in 1964. *Top right:* LP record carrying case, made by Airflite in 1964. It came out in red, blue or green. It measures 12½″x12½″. *Bottom left:* Disk-Go-Case made in 1966 by Charter Industries, U.S.A. Various colors were available, but brown is the rarest color. It is 8″ tall. *Bottom right:* Record carrying case, made by Airflite in 1964. Made to hold 45 records, the case came in red, blue or green. It measures 8½″x8″x5″.

BEATLES THREE RING BINDERS: These three ring binders were made in 1964. The white one was made by New York Looseleaf Corp. and the others were made by Standard Plastic Products. This shows every known color that was made.

THE BEATLES PLASTIC GUITARS: The plastic Beatles guitars were made in 1964 and are very hard to find, especially complete with the original packaging.

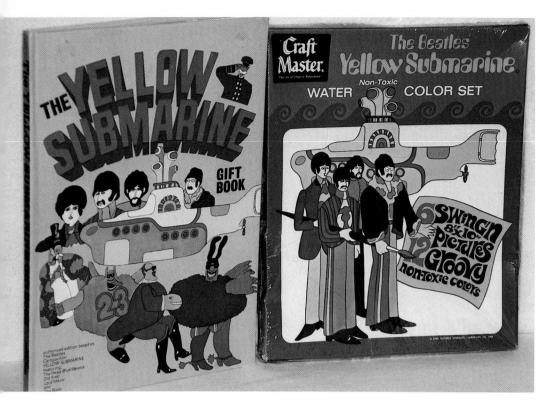

THE YELLOW SUBMARINE
GIFT BOOK AND WATER
COLOR SET: *The Yellow
Submarine* gift book was
published in 1968. *The
Yellow Submarine* water
color set was made in 1968
by Craft Master.

Left to right: Beatles guitar tie tack, made
in 1964 by Press Initial; *Yellow Submarine*
candy cigarette box and tray, made in
1968 by Primrose Confectionery; Set of
four candy cigarette boxes, made by
World Candies, Inc. in 1964; Beatles tie
tacks made in 1964 by Press Initial;
Brass and ceramic disk bracelet.

BEATLES LUNCH BOXES: *Top left:*
Kaboodle Kit, made by Standard Plastic
Products in 1964. *Top center:* Girls
brunchbag, made in 1965 by Aladdin.
Top right: Airflite lunchbox, made in
1964. *Bottom: Yellow Submarine,* made
by King Seely in 1968 and the blue lunch
box is made by Aladdin in 1965.

YELLOW SUBMARINE ANIMATION CELS: These are the original cels used in the movie *The Yellow Submarine*, which came out in 1968.

BEATLES HANDBAGS, PURSES AND PENCIL CASES: *Top row:* These handbags were all made in 1964. *Bottom left:* Yellow vinyl pencil case and red vinyl wallet, both made in 1964 by Standard Plastic Products. *Center:* Very rare, white vinyl handbag, made in 1964 by Airflite. It also came out in red. *Center front:* White vinyl cosmetic case, made in 1964. *Bottom right:* Clutch purse and pink wallet. Wallet contains comb, mirror, file and coin holder.

THE BEATLES YELLOW SUBMARINE POP-OUT ART DECORATIONS: The Beatles Yellow Submarine Pop-Out Art was made in 1968 and features twenty pop-out, standup characters from the movie *Yellow Submarine*. It measures 15″ by 10″.

BEATLES PINS, BUTTONS, RINGS AND TIE TACKS: *Top left:* Beatle Tie Tack, made in 1964 and guitar tie tack made in 1964. *Top center:* I Love the Beatles pin back button, measures 7" in diameter and was made in 1964; Plastic flasher rings made in 1964. *Top right:* Colored ceramic tie tack, made in 1964. *Top (far right):* Plastic guitar brooch, made in 1964. *Bottom left:* Two 3" buttons made in 1964. *Bottom center:* Three brass pins made in 1964. *Bottom right:* 3" pin back button made in 1964. *Bottom (far right):* Beatles fan club button measuring 3" in diameter.

BEATLE CALENDAR: This Beatles calendar was made in 1964 by John Fredrick Co., Illinois and is a rare salesman's sample with the original paperwork.

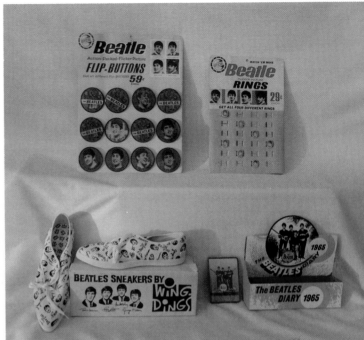

BEATLES PHONOGRAPH AND MODELS: The Beatles phonograph was made in 1964 by Craftmasters, measures 17½"x10" and operates at four speeds. *Top right:* The Yellow Submarine model kit was made in 1968 by Craftmaster. *Bottom row:* Beatles plastic model kits made by Revell in 1964.

BEATLES COLLECTIBLES: *Top left:* Flasher buttons, store display card. Made in 1964 by Saymore Co., Tennessee. It measures 14"x11". *Top right:* Flasher rings, store display card. Made in 1964 by Saymore Co., Tennessee. It measures 12"x8". *Bottom left:* Beatles Sneakers, made by Wing Dings in 1964. They came out in white or blue and they also made a high top version. *Bottom right:* The Beatles Diary and store display box were made in Scotland in 1965.

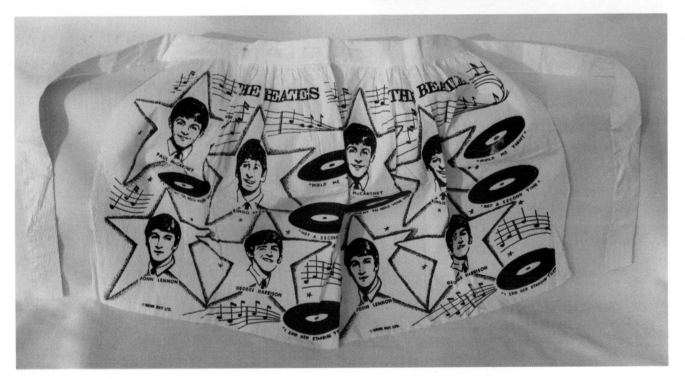

BEATLES APRON: This Beatles apron is made of paper and is very rare. It was made in 1964 by an unknown manufacturer.

BEATLES PILLOW: These pillows were made in 1964 by Nordic House, each measuring 12"x12". The hardest pillow to find is the one located in the bottom right hand corner (the standing version).

———————————

Bibliography

Frank, Alan, *Horror Films,* London: Hamlyn Publishing Group Limited, 1977.

Moran, Brian, *Battery Toys,* Schiffer Publishing Ltd., Atglen, Pennsylvania, 1984.

Sennett, Ted, *The Art of Hanna-Barbera,* Viking Studio Books.

Turpen, Carol, "Astronautical Toys," *Antique Toy World Magazine* 21:5, May 1991, pp. 76-81.

———— "The Creations of Hanna-Barbera," *Antique Toy World Magazine* 21:11, Nov. 1991, pp. 71-74.

———— "Futuristic Cars," *Antique Toy World Magazine* 22:2, Feb. 1992, pp. 124-127.

———— "Monster Toys," *Antique Toy World Magazine* 22:5, May 1992, pp. 148-151.

Price Guide

This book was put together to help the collector identify toys. The price guide will help give the collector a basic idea of how much a toy is worth, but prices vary across the country according to scarcity. The value of a toy is not necessarily the price a toy will sell for. Collectors have been known to pay outrageous prices for a certain toy that they have been unable to find to complete their collection. Prices in the Midwest differ from those in the West or East, and those at specialty shows will vary from those at general shows. And, of course, being at the right place at the right time can make all the difference.

All these factors make it impossible to create an absolutely accurate price list, but we can offer a guide. The prices quoted in this book are for unboxed toys that are in mint condition unless noted in the price guide. Toys that are priced as mint in the box will have m.i.b. next to the price. Boxed toys that are in mint condition bring a considerably higher price than those that are not in the original box. The prices should be set according to the condition of the toy. Generally, when a toy is repainted or restored the value decreases, although there are exceptions.

The left hand numbers are the page numbers. The names of the photographed items are in the center. The right hand numbers are the estimated prices or price ranges.

Page	Item	Price
7	Radicon Robot	4000-6000
7	Mechanized Robot	1800-2000
8	Rosko Astronaut	1800-2000
8	Lavender Robot	4000-6000
8	Train Robot	4000-6000
9	Cragstan Great Astronaut	1800
9	Door Robot	2000
10	Explo	150
10	Chief Robot Man	1200-1500
10	Man From Mars	300
11	Ratchet Robot	600
11	Space Explorer	1000-1500
11	Moon Explorer	2000
12	R-35 Robot	600
12	Flashy Jim	1000-1500
12	Robotank-Z	400
12	Dino Robot	800-900
13	Thunder Robot	3000-4000
13	Directional Robot	700-800
14	Space Robot (X-70)	800
14	Gear Robot	500
14	Cragstan Astronaut	1500
15	Space Commander	3000
15	Colonel Hap Hazard	800-900
15	Fighting Robot	200
16	Cragstan Ranger Robot	1000-1200
16	TV Spaceman	400-600
16	Forklift Robot	1800
17	Machine Robot	300
17	Cosmic Fighter	75-100
17	Engine Robot	150-200
18	Electric Robot	300
18	Attacking Martian	75-100
18	Mr. Robot	700-900
19	Zoomer the Robot	700
19	Mighty Robot With Spark	100
19	Spaceman	350
20	Space Scout	price unknown
20	Change Man Robot	price unknown
20	Mr. Patrol	500
21	Dalek	75-100
21	Robbie Robot	50
21	Space Explorer	1000-1500
22	Lost In Space Robot	100
22	Blink-A-Gear Robot	500-600
22	Television Spaceman	100-150
23	Man Made Satellite	150-200
23	Rendezvous 7 & 8	2000
24	Radicon Space Pathfinder	150-200
25	Outer Space Patrol	150
25	Zeroid Action Set	100-150
26	Orbit Explorer	500-600
26	Space Refuel Station	1800
27	Sonicon Rocket	500
27	Cragstan Space Tank	100-150
28	Radar Tank	175
28	Moon Detector	900-1200
28	Apollo II	150-200
29	Friendship 7	100-150
29	Moon Traveler Apollo Z	125
29	Super Apollo Space Capsule	100
30	Space Patrol X-ll	200-250
30	Space Patrol Tank	200
31	Moon Explorer	200
31	The Brain "Z Man"	175-250
31	Lunar Transport	150
32	Space Fighter	2000
32	Thunderbolt Special	50
32	Moon Orbiter	100
33	Lighted Space Vehicle	150-200
33	Super Moon Patroler	150
33	Space Ship X-5	50-75
34	Walking Space Patrol	150
34	Space Patrol R-lO	1500-1800
34	USA-NASA Gemini	175
35	Capsule 5	225
35	USA-NASA Apollo	75-100
36	Magic Color Mercury	150
36	Missile Boat	700
36	New Space Capsule	150
37	Bump'n Go Space Explorer	175
37	Magic Color Moon Express	125
38	Lost In Space Costume	150
38	Lost In Space Model	600-800
38	Space Orbitestor	75-125
39	Flying Jeep	150-200
39	Space Dog	300-350
39	Floating Satellite	75-125
40	Walking Frankenstein	1100-1500
41	Frankenstein Model	150-250
42	Mod Monster	150
42	Famous Monster Models	200-250
42	Frankenstein's Flivver	350
43	Wolfman	50
43	The Mummy	200-250
43	Wolfman's Wagon	350
44	Monster Scenes	75-150
44	Monsters of the Movies	75-150
45	Vampirella	150-175
45	Land of the Giants	250-350
46	Frankenstein Monster	150
46	Mighty Kong	250-300
47	Munsters Living Room	600-700
47	Grandpa Munster Puppet	75-100
47	Munsters Card Game	50-75
48	Munster Dolls	150-200
48	Munster Book	25
48	Munster Paper Dolls	75-100
48	Munster Coach	200
48	Munster Drag-u-la	200
49	Addams Family House	600-700
49	Lurch Doll	150-175
49	Gomez Puppet	75-100
50	Hamilton's Invaders	150-200
50	Witch Pitch	35
51	Famous Monsters repro.	5
51	Famous Monsters	10-15
51	Groovy Ghoulies	15-20
52	Li'l Coffin	75-100
52	Monster Vitamins	15
52	Roaring Gorilla	200-250
53	Gorilla	300-350
53	Creeple People	50-75
53	Jiras	300-400
54	Ford Fairlane 500	100
55	Firebird III	500-600
55	Firebird II	800-900
56	Firebird	300-500
56	Firebird III	400
56	Dream Car	400
57	Ford Gyron	200-250
57	Buick Le Sabre	400-500
57	Dream Car	1500-2000
58	Lincoln XL	350-400
58	Futuristic Car	200
58	Buick Phantom	700
59	The Lindberg	50-75
59	X-91 Futura	75-100
59	Futuristic Tootsietoys	60
60	Sea Hawk	200
60	Electromobile	100
61	VW Emergency Series	75
61	Citroen DS19	200-250
62	Dune Buggy	75
62	Dune Buggy and Camper	75
63	Wiking VWs	35
63	Smoking VW	75-100
64	King Size VW	150
64	Buddy L Truck	75
65	Raggedy Ann Camper	50
65	Musical Cadillac	150-200
65	Ford Thunderbird	125-150
66	Schucco 5503	250-300
66	Corvette Kit	50
66	Sound Bus	125
67	Tom and Jerry Roadster	250
67	BMW Isetta	150-200
68	Cadillac	125-150
68	VW Bus	250-300
69	Ford Mustang	100
70	U-Turn Cadallic	200
70	Go-Kart	250-300
70	'57 Chevy	75
71	7" Tin Car	50-75
71	T-Bird promo.	45
71	Desota promo.	75-100
71	Tonka Suburban	200
72	Johnny Lightening	65
72	Authentic Model Cars	125
72	Green Hornet Car	200
73	Monkeemobile	75
73	Dinky Kit	35
73	Hydraulic Aerial Ladder	250
74	Batman Helmet	75-100
75	Big Shot	75-100
76	Playmobile	200-250
76	Johnny Express	50-75
77	TV Jet	200-250
77	Big Bruiser	50-75
78	Flying Fox	225-300
78	Suzy Homemaker	25
78	Big Loo	700-800
79	Barbie Hot Hod	100-200
79	Army Truck	50
80	Captain Video Toy	800-1000
80	Sonar Sub Hunt	35
80	Aurora Derby	125
81	Robot Hands	150-200
81	Zeroids	50-100
81	Shangri-La City	75
82	The Visible Woman	40-50
82	Bonanza Figures	100
83	Nutty Generals	100
84	Nutty Mads M.I.P.	150
84	Series I	10-15
85	Series II	12-18
85	Series III	35-45
86	Nutty Mad Cars and Trikes	125-150
86	Nutty Mad Indian	100
87	Nutty Mad Target Game	150
87	Nutty Mad Car	200-250
87	Nutty Mad Boat/Car	75
87	Blame Its	35-50
88	Blame Its	35-50
88	Weird-ohs Model	30
89	Weird-ohs Figures	40-50
90	Magic Slate	35

No.	Item	Price
90	Drag Hag Model	150
90	Weird-ohs Game	150-200
91	MPC Weird-ohs	50
91	Weird-ohs Album	25
91	Rat Finks	5-10
92	Brother Rat Fink	75-100
92	Rat Fink Model	100
92	Hitler Model	150
92	Angel Fink	200-250
92	Robbin Hood Fink	400
93	Mother's Worry	100-125
93	Drag Nut	75-100
93	Mr Gasser	100
94	Baloon Blowing Bear	200 m.i.b.
95	Teddy The Artist	500-600 m.i.b.
96	Royal Cub	250 m.i.b.
96	Coffeetime Bear	200-250 m.i.b.
96	Picnic Bear	125 m.i.b.
96	Hungry Baby Bear	200-250 m.i.b.
97	The Jolly Peanut Vendor	350-425 m.i.b.
97	Bear The Shoe Maker	200-250 m.i.b.
97	Popcorn Vendor	350-450 m.i.b.
97	Sleeping Baby Bear	250-300 m.i.b.
98	Mother Bear	200-225 m.i.b.
98	Dentist Bear	650-750 m.i.b.
98	Telephone Bear	250 m.i.b.
99	Telephone Bear	250-300 m.i.b.
99	Blacksmith Bear	200-250 m.i.b.
99	Bear The Cashier	250-300 m.i.b.
100	Smoking Papa Bear	150-200 m.i.b.
100	Sneezing Bear	250-300 m.i.b.
100	The Drummer Boy	200-250 m.i.b.
101	Grand-Pa Panda Bear	250-300 m.i.b.
101	Teddy Bear Swing	350-400 m.i.b.
101	Shoe Shining Panda Bear	200-250 m.i.b.
101	Mighty Mike	300-350 m.i.b.
102	Blinky the Clown	250-300 m.i.b.
102	Ball Blowing Clown	200 m.i.b.
102	Drumming Clown	225 m.i.b.
102	Happy the Clown	300-350 m.i.b.
103	Charlie the Funny Clown	450-500 m.i.b.
103	Dozo the Steaming Clown	350-450 m.i.b.
103	Clown the Magician	250-300 m.i.b.
104	Jolly Bambino	300-375 m.i.b.
104	Suzette the Eating Monkey	900 m.i.b.
104	Bongo Monkey	200-225 m.i.b.
104	Trumpet Playing Monkey	200 m.i.b.
105	Jocko the Drinking Monkey	200 m.i.b.
105	Roller Skating Monkey	200-250 m.i.b.
105	Chimpy the Jolly Drummer	200-250 m.i.b.
105	Balloon Blowing Monkey	200-225 m.i.b.
106	Hy Que Monkey	500 m.i.b.
106	Dancing Merry Monkey	150-175 m.i.b.
106	Mischievous Monkey	500-600 m.i.b.
107	Picnic Monkey	350-450 m.i.b.
107	Space Traveling Monkey	175 m.i.b.
108	Bubble Blowing Monkey	200 m.i.b.
108	Chimp and Pup Rail Car	300 m.i.b.
108	Jumbo	100-125 m.i.b.
109	Bubble Bear	300-350 m.i.b.
109	Bubble Kangaroo	150-200 m.i.b.
109	Bubble Blowing Bunny	150-200 m.i.b.
110	Bubble Lion	125-175 m.i.b.
110	Bubble Blowing Musician	200-250 m.i.b.
110	Bubble Locomotive	50 m.i.b.
111	Mr. MacPooch	200-250 m.i.b.
111	Burger Chef	175-225 m.i.b.
111	Fido	350-400 m.i.b.
111	Dandy	200-250 m.i.b.
112	Musical Bulldog	1800-2000 m.i.b.
112	Buttons	250 m.i.b.
112	Playful Puppy	200-250 m.i.b.
113	Rabbit and Carriage	250-325 m.i.b.
113	Telephone Rabbit	200-275 m.i.b.
113	Cappy the Baggage Porter	250-300 m.i.b.
114	Picnic Bunny	125-175 m.i.b.
114	Peter the Drumming Rabbit	225 m.i.b.
114	Grasshopper	200 m.i.b.
114	Talking Parrot	550-600 m.i.b.
115	Drinking Licking Cat	350 m.i.b.
115	Dennis the Menace	400-450 m.i.b.
115	Ol' Sleepy Head Rip	400-450 m.i.b.
116	Feeding Bird Watcher	450 m.i.b.
116	Two Gun Sheriff	200-250 m.i.b.
116	Major Tooty	150-200 m.i.b.
117	Captain Blushwell	100 m.i.b.
117	McGregor	150-200 m.i.b.
117	Drinking Captain	100-150 m.i.b.
117	Good Time Charlie	250-300 m.i.b.
118	Mexicali Pete	200-225 m.i.b.
118	Switchboard Operator	400 m.i.b.
118	Sam the Shaving Man	325 m.i.b.
119	Hamburger Chef	125-150 m.i.b.
119	Strutting My Fair Dancer	200-225 m.i.b.
119	Climbing Linesman	500-600 m.i.b.
120	Smoking Grandpa	200-225 m.i.b.
120	Arthur A-Go-Go Drummer	750-850 m.i.b.
120	Puffy Morris	100-125 m.i.b.
121	Snake Charmer	400-500 m.i.b.
121	Western Bad Man	650-750 m.i.b.
122	Mr. Baseball Jr.	750-850 m.i.b.
122	Roulette	200-250 m.i.b.
122	Pinocchio	300-350 m.i.b.
123	Indian Joe	150 m.i.b.
123	Traffic Policeman	425 m.i.b.
123	Happy Santa	200 m.i.b.
124	Santa on Rotating Globe	550-650 m.i.b.
124	Santa Claus	350-400 m.i.b.
124	Santa & Space Scooter	200 m.i.b. each
125	Space Patrol	175-250 m.i.b.
125	Kissing Couple	250-300 m.i.b.
125	Fire Chief Car	300-375 m.i.b.
126	Turn-O-Matic Gun Jeep	150 m.i.b.
126	Highway Patrol	1000-1200 m.i.b.
126	Fire Chief Car No. 7	300-375 m.i.b.
126	Fire Tricycle	500-600 m.i.b.
127	Police Patrol Jeep	250 m.i.b.
127	Battle Helicopter	100-125 m.i.b.
128	Police Helicopter	200-250 m.i.b.
128	Whistling Show Boat	175 m.i.b.
129	Douglas DC-9 Jet Plane	150-225 m.i.b.
129	Multi-Action Electra Jet	250-300 m.i.b.
129	Take-Off and Landing Jet	300-375 m.i.b.
130	Boeing 747 Jet Plane	35-50 m.i.b.
130	Pan Am Boeing 747	25-40 m.i.b.
131	Porsche Carrera	75-100
131	Firebird Speedway Racer	250-300
132	Jet Racer	300-400
132	Porsche Racer	50-100
132	Porsche 917K	100-150
133	VW Porsche 914	100
133	Distler Porsche	500
134	Comet Racer	75-100
134	Jet Racer	100-150
135	Mercedes Racer	300
135	International Stock Car	75-125
136	Ferrari 250/Lemans	100-150
136	Ferrari 365GT BB	150
136	Lamborghini Countach	150
137	Chaparral 2F	200
137	Firestone Race Car	75-125
138	BMW 3.5 CSL Turbo	75-100
138	Rallye Race Car Set	150
139	Stunt Car	200-250
139	Champion Midget Racer	500-700
139	Rocket Racer	150-200
139	Porsche	100-150
140	Mercedes Racer	300-350
140	Corvette	75
140	Race Car	100
141	Porsche 911 S	125
141	Big Stunt Car	75-100
142	Go-Stop Benz Racer	200-300
142	Ford G.T. 40	150
143	TV-Tinykins	500-600
144	Flintstone Tinykins	50-100 each
144	TV-Tinykins	50-100 each
144	TV-Tinykins	50-100 each
145	TV Play Set & TV Scenes	50-100 each
145	Tom & Jerry Locomotive	150-200
146	Tom & Jerry Hand Car	150-200
146	Flintstone Dakins	30 each
147	Fred & Bamm Bamm	25-35 each
148	Flintstone Truck	600-700
148	Rubble's Wreck & Flivver	650-700 each
148	Flintstone Cars	150-200 each
149	Flintstone Car	200-300
150	Flintstone Bedrock Express	350-400
150	Flintstone Tricycle	300-400 each
151	Fred Flintstone on Dino	600-700
152	Fred on Dino & Pals	300-400 each
152	Dino-the-Dinosaur	600-800
152	Hopping Fred & Barney	300-350 each
153	Flintstone Turnover Tank	400-500
154	Slant Walkers	40-75 each
154	Hanna-Barbera Push Ups	20-25 each
154	Bedrock Band	300-400
155	Spinikin	20-25
155	TV Guides	15-25
155	Flintstones Record	20-25
155	Paper Dolls	40-50
156	Rocky	100-125
156	Pull Toys	300-400 each
156	Pixie & Dixie Ceramic Figure	price unknown
156	H-Barbera Ceramic Figures	25-35 each
157	Yogi Bear	35-75
158	Wall Plaques	35-50 each
158	Quick Draw McGraw	30-40
158	Touche Turtle	30-40
159	Magilla Gorilla	35-75 each
160	Squeak Toys	25-35 each
160	Magilla Gorilla	35-75
160	Huckleberry Hound	25-35
161	Magilla Gorilla	25-35
162	Yogi & H'berry Squeak Toys	25-35 each
162	Yogi Bear Squeak Toy	25-35
162	Tricky Trapeze	20-25
162	Push Up Puppets	20-25 each
163	Go-Mobiles	300-350 each
163	Huckleberry Cars	150 each
164	Animal Airplane	500-600
164	Hopping Toys	300-350 each
164	Slant Walkers	40-75 each
165	Push Button Puppets	20-25 each
165	Quick Draw Pull Toy	no value
166	Jetson Hopping Toys	300-400 each
166	Jetson Express	400-450
166	Jetsons Turnover Tank	350-400
167	Scooby Doo Squeak Toy	25-35
167	Spike Squeak Toy	25-35
167	Jetson Slant Walkers	40-75 each
168	Hair Bear Squeak Toys	25-40 each
168	Hari Bear Plush Toy	35-75
169	Happy Life	175
170	Rocking Dog	50
171	Skip Rope Animals	150
171	Bouncing Dolly Ball	65
171	Suzy Bouncing Ball	65
172	Monkey Carousel	75
172	Sea Wolf	100-125
172	Vacationland Airplane	125
173	Tom Tom Jungle Boy	225
174	Squirrel Land	100
174	Rollerskating Clown	200
175	Cubby the Reading Bear	75
175	Skippy the Cyclist	150
175	Little Monkey Shiner	65
176	Milton Berle Car	350
177	Donkey Boy	35-50
177	Mechanical Fur Monkey	50
178	Casey Jr.	200
178	Circus Parade	150
179	Happy Grandpa	50
179	Helicopter	75
180	Bicycle Windup	100
180	Disney Whirlygig	price unknown
180	Comic Helicopter	50-75
181	Flapping Butterfly	75-100
181	Grandpas New Car	200
182	Rare Beatles Book Binder	175-250
182	6" Beatles Bowl	75-125
182	Yellow Submarine, Corgi	300-400
182	Plastic Tumbler	35-70
182	Plastic Mug	65-125
182	Beatles Bath Containers	90
182	Beatles Dolls	35-75
182	Harmonica	70-100
183	Yellow Submarine Clock	350-500
183	Insulated Glass	175
183	Talcum Powder	300-500
183	Perfume	price unknown
183	Beatles Hair Spray	600-900
183	Yellow Submarine Candle	300-500
184	Overnight Bag	275-425
184	LP Record Carrying Case	175-350
184	Disk-Go-Case	75-125
184	45 Record Carrying Case	125-300
185	Beatles Three Ring Binders	75-200
185	Beatles Plastic Guitars	250-600
186	Yellow Submarine Gift Book	75
186	Water Color Set	75
186	Guitar Tie Tack	20
186	Candy Cigarette Box & Tray	150
186	Four Candy Cigarette Boxes	50-100 each
186	Four Tie Tacks	25 each
186	Bracelet	75
186	Kaboodle Kit	400-800
186	Girls Brunchbag	250-450
186	Airflite Lunchbox	400-700
186	Yellow Submarine Lunchbox	250-400
186	Blue Lunchbox	250-400
187	Yellow Submarine Cels	500-1000 each
187	Pop-Out Art Decorations	75
187	Beatles Handbags	250-400
187	Yellow Pencil Case	125
187	Red & Pink Wallets	75-125
187	White Vinyl Handbag	500+
187	White Cosmetic Case	150-250
187	Clutch Purse	150-250
188	Four Tie Tacks	25-35
188	Guitar Tie Tack	25
188	7" Pinback Button	100-150
188	Four Flasher Rings	40-50 set
188	Ceramic Tie Tack	75-100
188	Plastic Guitar Broach	15-25
188	3" Buttons	15-25
188	Brass Pins	45-75
188	Fan Club Button	12
188	Salesman Sample Calender	price unknown
189	Phonograph	800-1400
189	Yellow Submarine Model	150-250
189	Model Kits	150-225
189	Flasher Buttons	200-350
189	Flasher Rings	200-350
189	Sneakers	300-475
189	Diary	25
189	Store Display Box	35-75
189	Beatles Apron	price unknown
190	Beatles Pillow	75-250